A Look at Regional Differences
in American Sign Language

SIGNS ACROSS AMERICA

Edgar H. Shroyer
and
Susan P. Shroyer

GALLAUDET COLLEGE PRESS
Washington, D.C.

Gallaudet College Press
Washington, DC 20002

©1984 by Gallaudet College. All rights reserved
Published 1984
Printed in the United States of America

Gallaudet College is an equal opportunity employer/educational institution. Programs
and services offered by Gallaudet College receive substantial financial support from the
U.S. Department of Education.

To
Patricia (Trish)
and
Jeffrey

CONTENTS

PREFACE

What's your sign for . . .? Most people associated with deafness and signing have heard or asked this question many times. In fact, this simple interrogative often initiates a period of sharing various signs for selected words that each of us has seen in a particular school, city, or state. Most people who sign enjoy this sharing of signs that they have seen or used, and many often adopt a new sign due to this exposure.

Many of us have changed the way we traditionally or first learned to sign particular words as a result of a geographic move or even a change in employment. Generally, we try to integrate regional or local signs into our communication to be more readily understood by those around us. As our exposure to various signs grows, it is fun and satisfying to sit back, appreciate, and marvel at the myriad of differences and subtleties of signing. Without fail, specific signs stick with us and we tend to show and compare them with others who have the same interest in signs. Our interest in sharing signs gave birth to the concept of *Signs Across America*.

The primary purpose of this book is to record and share with others the different signs for selected words that we collected from people in 25 different states. In addition, we hope this book will help to ensure the preservation of some of the more traditional signs that may be forgotten because of the use of more and more Manually Coded English signs.

Most sign books are reference or instructional texts comprised of the more widely accepted signs. These books are designed either for beginning students or sign interpreters trying to improve their vocabulary and skills. We feel *Signs Across America* is an innovative, fun book that will be of interest to these groups as well as teachers of signs, deaf individuals, linguists, and researchers.

The Selection Process

We began this project by compiling a list of 160 English words for which we and some friends associated with deafness and signing knew at least two different signs for the same concept. No thought was given to the number of nouns, verbs, adjectives, or other parts of speech. We then contacted native signers in four different states to show us the American Sign Language (ASL) or traditional sign they would use to express the concept represented by each word in a contextual sentence. Contributors were asked to avoid using Manually Coded English signs.

After receiving this data, we reduced our list to 130 words. The main criterion for including a word was that we received at least three different signs for each concept.

In order to get a representative sampling of signs from across the United States, we contacted various people in selected states. They agreed to help us get the signs from individuals they felt had a good knowledge of the signs in their states. We collected signs from 25 states. We felt these states represented a good cross section of the country. We attempted to contact individuals from those states having sizable deaf populations, while at the same time considering the regions of the country those states represented.

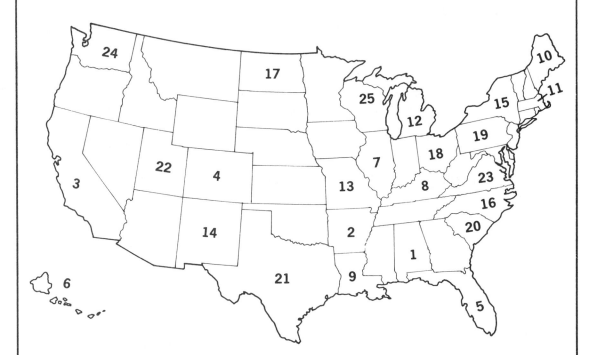

States Represented in *Signs Across America*

1. Alabama
2. Arkansas
3. California
4. Colorado
5. Florida
6. Hawaii
7. Illinois
8. Kentucky
9. Louisiana
10. Maine
11. Massachusetts
12. Michigan
13. Missouri
14. New Mexico
15. New York
16. North Carolina
17. North Dakota
18. Ohio
19. Pennsylvania
20. South Carolina
21. Texas
22. Utah
23. Virginia
24. Washington
25. Wisconsin

Profile of Contributors

Thirty-eight people provided us with signs from their particular states. The age range of the contributors was 25 to 86 years, with a mean of 50.3 years. Only two of the contributors are hearing. The number of years that each person had lived in their representative state ranged from 10 to 83 years, with a mean of 44.5 years. The number of years that each individual had been deaf at the time of taping ranged from 25 to 83 years, with a mean of 52.6. (These latter figures do not include the two contributors who are hearing.) The number of years that the contributors have been signing ranged from 4 (an adventitiously deafened person) to 79 years, with a mean of 45.6 years.

The individuals who served as contributors represented what we considered a very good cross section of the deaf population. We had contributors who worked in residential schools for the deaf, community service centers, and interpreter training programs; several contributors were employed in nonprofessional positions, and a few were retired. We attempted to avoid individuals associated with educational settings because of their tendency to use more Manually Coded English signs. We also did not include black deaf signs in our research because of the many differences between black and white signs in the southern states. This area has been researched and been reported in the literature on signing (see Woodward, 1976a).

Sign Variations

Some contributors gave us more than one sign for a single concept; therefore, more than one sign illustration may be shown for some states. In other instances, two different contributors from the same state gave us two different signs for the same concept. We tried to faithfully represent all of the signs from the various contributors. However, we realize that these are not necessarily the signs used by everyone residing in a particular state. Just as there are differences between states, there are also differences within states. Signs often vary from city to city or between various areas within a state, and it would have been a monumental, if not impossible, task to include all the variations within a state. Therefore, we assume all responsibility for the signs shown in this book. We hope people from the various states represented in this book will enjoy seeing variations of signs within their own state even if these signs may not be signs that they themselves employ.

It is interesting to note the variety of handshapes, locations, movements, and hand orientations among the signs for the same word. Some of these differ in all respects, as can be seen in the signs for *picnic* on the following page.

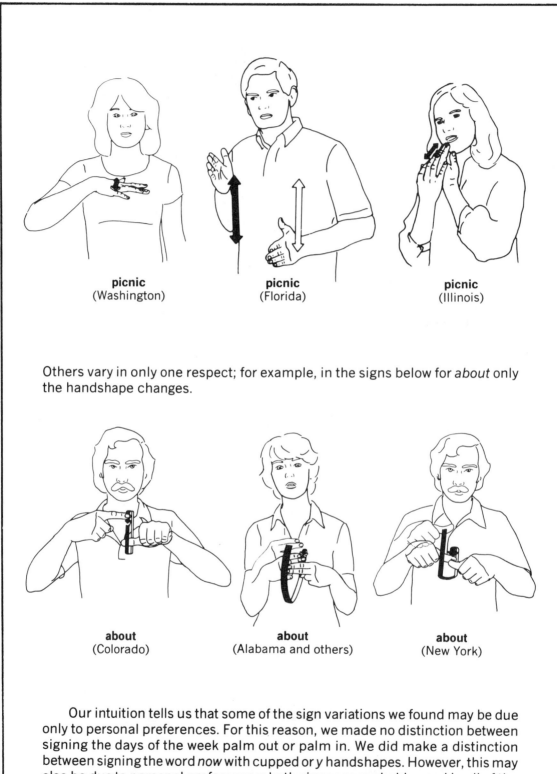

picnic
(Washington)

picnic
(Florida)

picnic
(Illinois)

Others vary in only one respect; for example, in the signs below for *about* only the handshape changes.

about
(Colorado)

about
(Alabama and others)

about
(New York)

Our intuition tells us that some of the sign variations we found may be due only to personal preferences. For this reason, we made no distinction between signing the days of the week palm out or palm in. We did make a distinction between signing the word *now* with cupped or *y* handshapes. However, this may also be due to personal preferences; both signs are probably used in all of the states. The only state showing a completely different sign for *now* was Hawaii. (A possible explanation for this is offered in the introduction.)

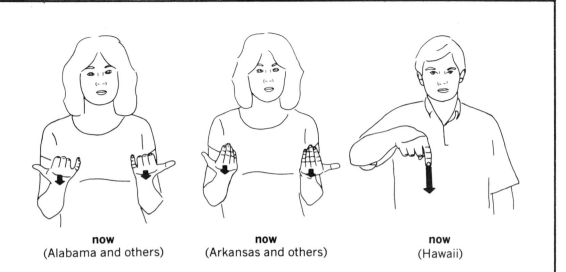

now
(Alabama and others)

now
(Arkansas and others)

now
(Hawaii)

While compiling the information for this book, we did give some thought to adding a section on possible sign origins, but we quickly decided that such an undertaking would be overwhelming and ultimately meaningless. It appears most signers can only make an educated guess concerning sign origins, and consensus in this area is next to impossible. Speculations do exist, however, and we have included three of ours.

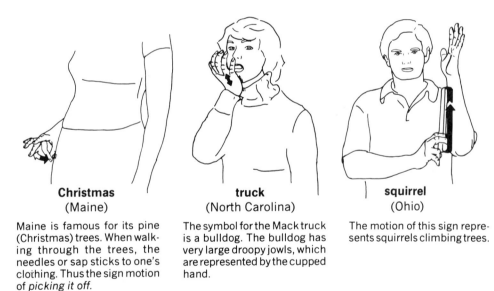

Christmas
(Maine)

truck
(North Carolina)

squirrel
(Ohio)

Maine is famous for its pine (Christmas) trees. When walking through the trees, the needles or sap sticks to one's clothing. Thus the sign motion of *picking it off.*

The symbol for the Mack truck is a bulldog. The bulldog has very large droopy jowls, which are represented by the cupped hand.

The motion of this sign represents squirrels climbing trees.

We have enjoyed working with the many people who helped compile this book. And, we have been fascinated with the numbers and kinds of sign variations we have seen. We originally estimated we would find 800 signs for our selected vocabulary. We were surprised to find there were approximately 1200 variations for these 130 words. Everyone with whom we have shared these variations has found them interesting, funny, weird, and informative. We hope you share these feelings.

ACKNOWLEDGMENTS

Compiling a book of such complexity and scope as *Signs Across America* required the assistance of many different individuals. We want to express our gratitude and appreciation to all of them for their knowledge, time, patience, and especially, their willingness to contribute to this book. The names of all those individuals who were videotaped while providing us with signs from their respective states are listed below. Not listed, but to whom we are equally grateful, are those individuals who contacted our deaf signers, operated cameras, gave technical advice, and coordinated the project in their states. Without their combined efforts, *Signs Across America* would not have come to fruition. Thank you.

Peggy Baird
Celia May Baldwin
Homer Beekman
Ruth Beekman
Nancy Benedetto
Anna Buckner
Raymond Buckner
Daniel Burch
Rita Campbell
Comos Caragliano
Jennie Caragliano
Robert Clingenpeel
Jewell Coots
Charles Crandall
Shannon Crandall
Susan Crouch
Terri Crump
Denzil R. Fewell
Lillian Florence

Richard Frazer
Lillian Hoshauer
Elinor L. Kraft
Linda Lambrecht
Diana Maupin
April Nelson
Arlene W. Nelson
Germaine Pinette
Ronald Pinette
Marilyn Rafferty
Inez Rause
Joe Sarpy
James Schooley
Helen Shroyer
Virgil Shroyer
Robert Swan
Mike Tuccelli
Henry G. Walls
Evelyn Zola

We would also like to thank our friends who served with us as models, typists, and advisors. Michelle Blevins and Cindy King fall into the latter categories. They both spent considerable time at the computer and made many helpful suggestions. Ivey Pittle deserves special thanks for her assistance and advice in the final stages of the book. Our models for the illustrations are shown on the opposite page. Each of them willingly donated hours of his or her own time, and they all provided us with valuable input for this book.

Terri Crump

Donald Crump

Marcy Maury

Richard Thornberry

Susan Shroyer

Edgar Shroyer

INTRODUCTION

Signing has been a part of the deaf community as long as deafness has existed. As a national leader in the deaf community once said many years ago, "As long as there are deaf people there will be signing." It is recognized and generally accepted that Thomas Hopkins Gallaudet, a hearing American clergyman, and Laurent Clerc, a deaf French educator of deaf children, established the first permanent school for the deaf in the United States in 1817. They brought together deaf children from a variety of places in New England to their school (now known as the American School for the Deaf) in Hartford, Connecticut. This was the children's first exposure to formal education. Clerc, who was fluent in French Sign Language, introduced his signs in this newly established school.

It would be rather naive of anyone to think that these two men are solely responsible for introducing signs in America. Clerc is reported to have frequently complained to friends that his students were not using all of the signs that he showed them. They were, according to him, changing some of his "beautiful French signs" as well as stubbornly using signs that they had brought to the school with them.

Clerc's complaints serve as one indication that signs were obviously used by deaf individuals in America prior to 1817. Further evidence can be found in Groce's research (1980) on an established sign language used on Martha's Vineyard beginning in the seventeenth century. Many of the children from Martha's Vineyard attended the school in Hartford. Current research also shows that deaf children of hearing parents make up signs to communicate with their parents and siblings. Young deaf children in schools that forbid signing are frequently seen signing to one another outside of school. There appears to be little doubt that deaf people have indeed, historically, always used signs to communicate with one another as well as with individuals who are not deaf.

If deaf people originally invented many of their own signs, then it seems logical that deaf people from New England would not be able to communicate with deaf people living in Ohio. Around the early 1800s they probably could not. Today, a deaf traveler going across America would have very little, if any, difficulty conversing with other deaf people encountered along the way. There may be an occasional sign that the traveler might not know, but context would probably clarify the sign's meaning.

The ability of deaf people from different areas of the country to communicate without any difficulty has to be attributed to Clerc and Gallaudet. The signs that they taught were carried by graduates of their school to other parts of the country. Several people trained at the American School were instrumental in establishing schools for the deaf in different parts of the country. Consequently, the signs taught at the American School were in turn taught to children and others associated with deaf people in other parts of the United States.

Still, the spread of these signs did not result in a complete change in the signs that deaf people elsewhere used. Although this new sign language gained considerable social and educational prestige, many of the local and regional signs were retained and then assimilated into the language. This merger of local signs with Clerc's French signs was one step in the evolution of American Sign Language. The retention of local signs may account for some of the variations we found. However, many of the signs invented for communication prior to the arrival of French Sign Language are, unfortunately, lost forever.

Sign language in Hawaii seems to have developed without the influence of Clerc and Gallaudet. Hawaii's distance from the mainland caused a considerable delay in the establishment of formal education for deaf people on the islands. Therefore, they were not exposed to the signs carried to most other places by the disciples of Clerc and Gallaudet. Readers will note that many of the Hawaiian signs do not follow the principles of American Sign Language.

Individuals involved with signing today have to stop and wonder what kinds of changes are occurring now. The current trend of using new signing systems (i.e., Manually Coded English) in schools for the deaf and teacher-training programs throughout the country is undoubtedly taking its toll on many of the more traditional signs. Many of the more traditional signs are not being used because there are fewer and fewer people involved in education who know these signs to perpetuate them. On the other hand, one could argue that because sign language is a dynamic, living language, change is inevitable. It does seem to be a shame, though, to lose what many people feel to be a very important part of our deaf heritage.

Suggested Readings

Baker, C., & Cokely, D. (1980). *American Sign Language: A teacher's resource text on grammar and culture.* Silver Spring, MD: T.J. Publishers, Inc.

Croneberg, C.G. (1965). Sign language dialects. In W.C. Stokoe, Jr., D.C. Casterline, & C.G. Croneberg (Eds.), *Dictionary of American Sign Language on linguistic principles.* Washington, DC: Gallaudet College Press.

Fant, L. (1974). Ameslan. *Gallaudet Today*, Winter, 5.

Friedman, L. (1977). *On the other hand: New perspectives on American Sign Language.* New York: Academic Press.

Gannon, J.R. (1981). *Deaf heritage: A narrative history of deaf America.* Silver Spring, MD: National Association of the Deaf.

Green, K. (1984). Sign boundaries in American Sign Language. *Sign Language Studies, 42*, 65-91.

Groce, N. (1980). Everyone spoke sign language here: Martha's Vineyard. *Deaf American, 33*(2), 3-6.

Hoemann, H. (1978). *Communicating with deaf people.* Baltimore, MD: University Park Press.

Kantor, R. (1980). The acquisition of classifiers in American Sign Language. *Sign Language Studies, 28*, 193-208.

Klima, E., & Bellugi, U. (1979). *The signs of language.* Cambridge, MA: Harvard University Press.

Stedt, J., & Moores, D. (1980). The etymology of an esoteric sign. *Sign Language Studies, 29*, 371-376.

Stokoe, W. (1971). *The study of sign language.* Silver Spring, MD: National Association of the Deaf.

Wilbur, R. (1979). *American Sign Language and sign systems.* Baltimore, MD: University Park Press.

Woodward, J.C., Jr. (1975). Synchronic variation and historical change in American Sign Language. *Language Science, 37*, 9-12.

Woodward, J.C., Jr. (1976a). Black southern signing. *Language Science, 5*, 211-218.

Woodward, J.C., Jr. (1976b). Signs of change: Historical variations in American Sign Language. *Sign Language Studies, 10*, 81-94.

Woodward, J.C., Jr. (1978). Historical bases of American Sign Language. In P. Siple (Ed.), *Understanding language through sign language research* (pp. 333-348). New York: Academic Press.

Woodward, J.C., Jr. (1980). Sociolinguistic research on American Sign Language: An historical perspective. In C. Baker & R. Battison (Eds.), *Sign language and the deaf community* (pp. 117-134). Silver Spring, MD: National Association of the Deaf.

FORMAT

The format of the book is quite simple in that the 130 vocabulary entries are arranged alphabetically. Each new entry is enclosed in a box. A sentence that clarifies the meaning of the entry is also included in the box. The sign illustrations following the box are presented in alphabetical order according to state.

Some contributors showed us two or more signs for a particular word within a state. We indicated this in parentheses after the state with *1 of 2* and *2 of 2* or *1 of 3*, *2 of 3*, and *3 of 3* so that readers will know to look for more than one sign in that particular state. In many instances we found that the sign for a word in one state was the same as the sign for a different word in another state. We did not find any explanations for the similarities, but we do want readers to be aware of them.

If our contributor did not know or use a sign for the word, we indicated that the word is fingerspelled. Occasionally, someone would show us a sign and at the same time say that some people had no sign for that particular concept, so they fingerspelled the English equivalent. Since this can be done with all words, we decided to include only the sign that was shown. In a few cases an abbreviation for a word was given rather than a sign. This coincides with current research in signing that some abbreviated words are, in effect, the word's "sign." Examples of this are found in Michigan, which showed *f-a-v* for *favorite*, and in Wisconsin, which fingerspelled *straw* and signed *berry*.

All of our models in the illustrations are right handed, so the right hand is to be considered the dominant hand in all two-handed signs. Many of the signs involve more than one movement (i.e., a change in the location, handshape, or direction). In some cases we indicated movement by adding 1 to the first position and 2 to the second, or final, position. In other cases, the first position is drawn with a fine line and the final position with a heavy line.

Almost all of the two-handed signs support the finding that if the hand-shapes of both hands are similar, both hands move (fig. 1). If the handshapes are different, only the dominant hand moves (fig. 2).

Fig. 1. pear

Fig. 2. picture

The arrows also assist you in making this decision. When there are two arrows showing the same movement but one is black and the other white, the hands move in opposition (fig. 3). When two black arrows show the same movement, the hands move in the same direction (fig. 4).

Fig. 3. worry

Fig. 4. delicious

A black curved arrow with two points indicates a shaking movement (fig. 5). A black and white curved arrow with two points indicates a twisting movement (fig. 6).

Fig. 5. purple

Fig. 6. hearing aid

A black and white arrow indicates an opening and closing motion (figs. 7 and 8). The other arrows indicating movement should be readily understood. Small shading marks are used to indicate that the hands touch another part of the body or hands (fig. 9).

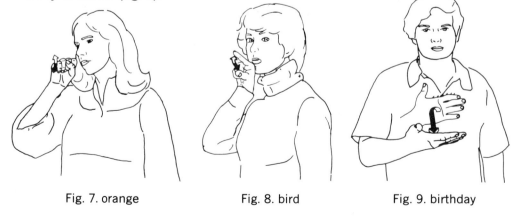

Fig. 7. orange

Fig. 8. bird

Fig. 9. birthday

SIGN
ENTRIES

about

Tell me about your friend.

1 Alabama, Louisiana, North Carolina

2 Arkansas, Florida, Illinois, Kentucky, South Carolina, Texas, Utah, Wisconsin

3 California, Maine, Massachusetts, Missouri, New Mexico, New York (1 of 2), North Dakota, Pennsylvania, Virginia

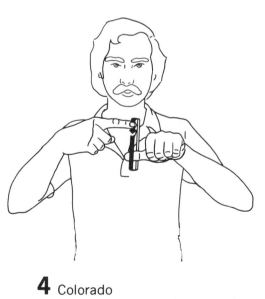

4 Colorado

about

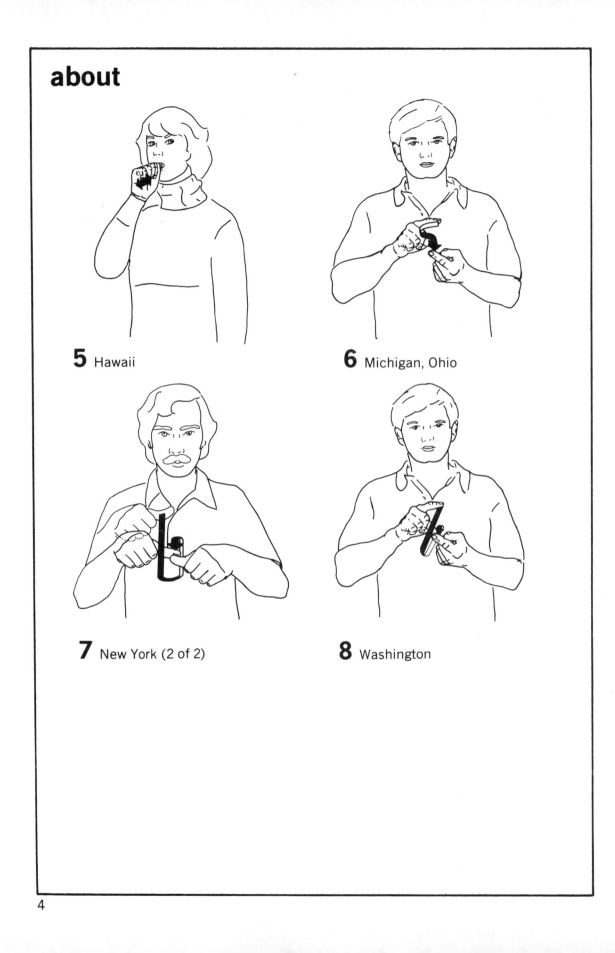

5 Hawaii

6 Michigan, Ohio

7 New York (2 of 2)

8 Washington

airport

We waited at the airport for one hour before our plane took off.

FINGERSPELL: Alabama, South Carolina

1 Arkansas

2 California, Colorado, Hawaii, Kentucky, Louisiana, Massachusetts, Michigan, Missouri (1 of 2), New York, North Dakota, Ohio, Pennsylvania, Washington, Wisconsin

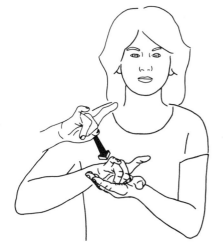

3 Florida, Illinois, Missouri (2 of 2)

4 Maine

5

airport

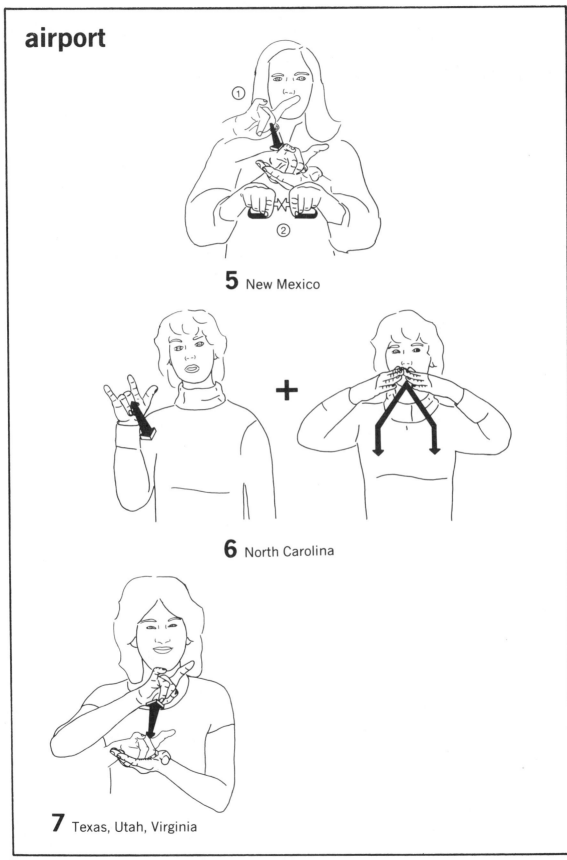

5 New Mexico

6 North Carolina

7 Texas, Utah, Virginia

apple

We sold 50 apple pies at the bake sale.

1 Alabama

2 Arkansas

3 California, Colorado, Florida, Illinois, Massachusetts (1 of 2), Michigan, Missouri, New Mexico, New York, North Dakota, Ohio, South Carolina, Texas, Utah, Virginia, Washington, Wisconsin

4 Hawaii

apple

5 Kentucky, Maine, North Carolina

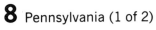

6 Louisiana

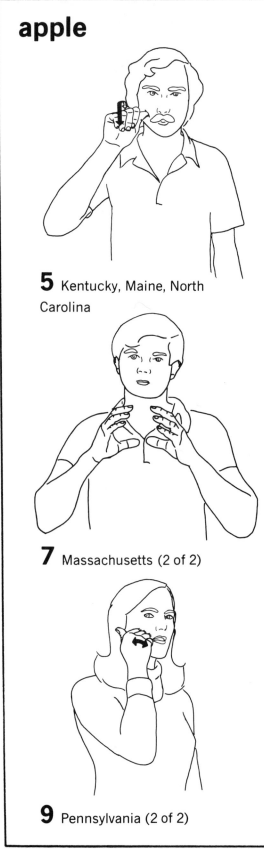

7 Massachusetts (2 of 2)

8 Pennsylvania (1 of 2)

9 Pennsylvania (2 of 2)

arrest

Did the police arrest her?

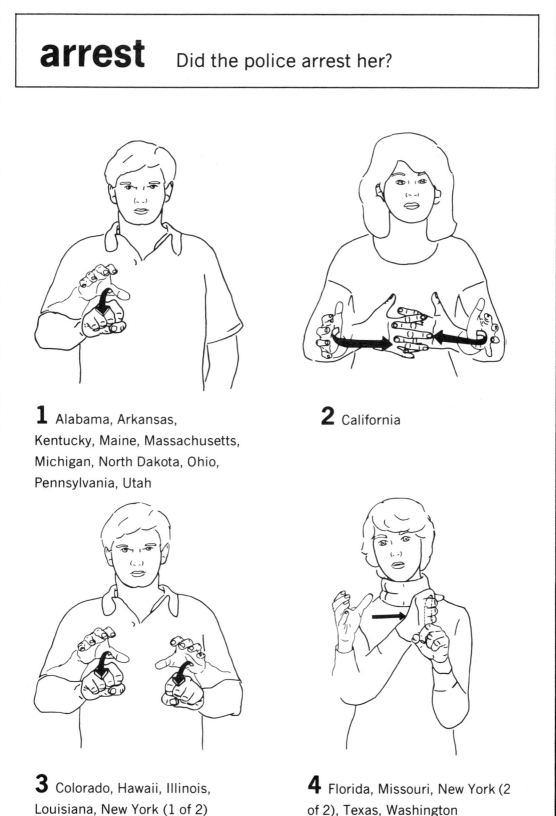

1 Alabama, Arkansas, Kentucky, Maine, Massachusetts, Michigan, North Dakota, Ohio, Pennsylvania, Utah

2 California

3 Colorado, Hawaii, Illinois, Louisiana, New York (1 of 2)

4 Florida, Missouri, New York (2 of 2), Texas, Washington

arrest

5 New Mexico

6 North Carolina

7 South Carolina, Virginia

8 Wisconsin

banana

Monkeys love to eat bananas.

1 Alabama

2 Arkansas, Illinois, Kentucky, Louisiana, Michigan, Missouri, North Carolina (1 of 2)

3 California, New Mexico, Utah, Washington

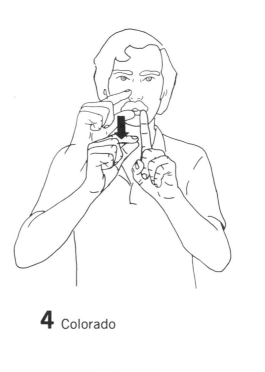

4 Colorado

banana

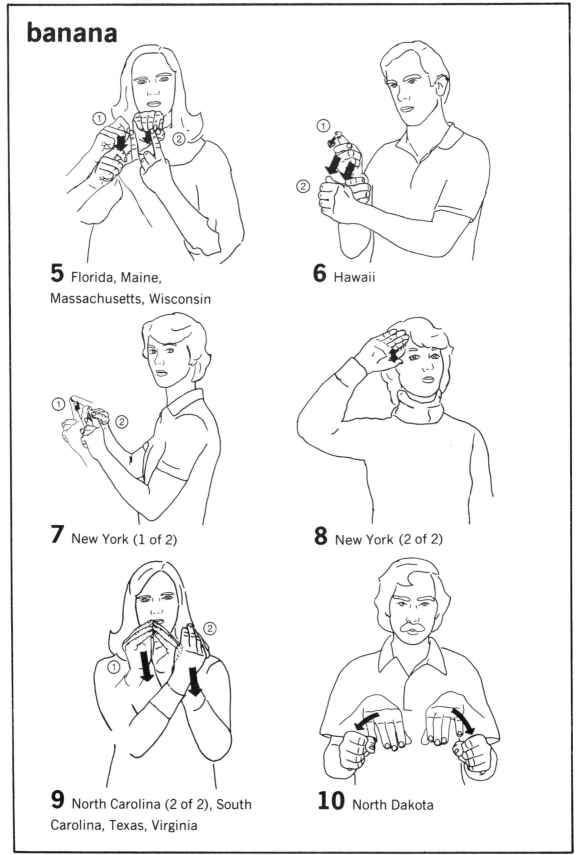

5 Florida, Maine, Massachusetts, Wisconsin

6 Hawaii

7 New York (1 of 2)

8 New York (2 of 2)

9 North Carolina (2 of 2), South Carolina, Texas, Virginia

10 North Dakota

11 Ohio

12 Pennsylvania (1 of 3)

13 Pennsylvania (2 of 3)

14 Pennsylvania (3 of 3)

bathroom

He hates to clean the bathroom.

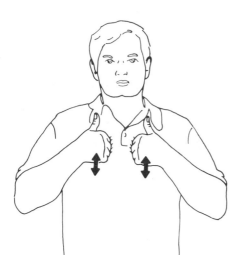

1 Alabama, Louisiana, Michigan, North Dakota

2 Arkansas (1 of 2), California, Illinois (1 of 2), Kentucky, Massachusetts, Missouri (1 of 2), New Mexico, New York (1 of 2), North Carolina, Pennsylvania (1 of 4), Utah, Virginia, Washington

3 Arkansas (2 of 2)

4 Colorado, Illinois (2 of 2), Pennsylvania (2 of 4), South Carolina, Texas, Wisconsin

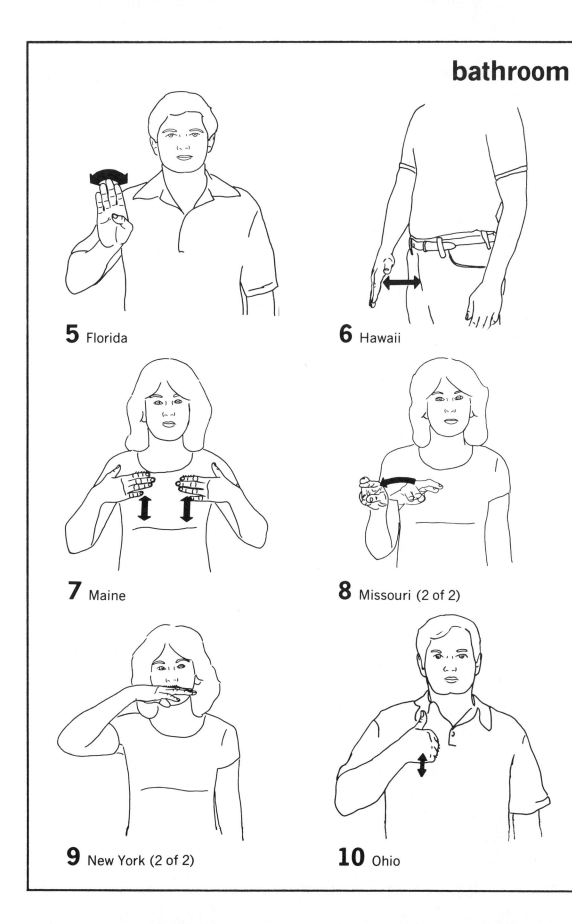

bathroom

5 Florida

6 Hawaii

7 Maine

8 Missouri (2 of 2)

9 New York (2 of 2)

10 Ohio

bathroom

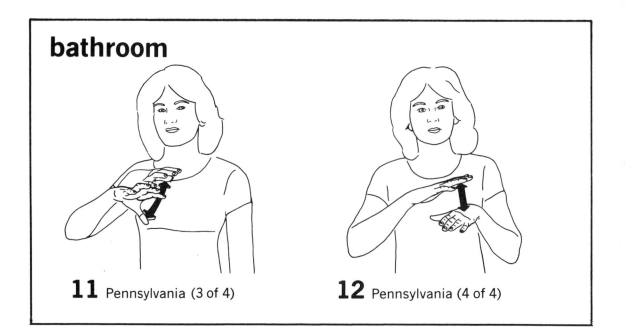

11 Pennsylvania (3 of 4) **12** Pennsylvania (4 of 4)

beer Is the beer cold?

FINGERSPELL: Alabama, Utah, Virginia

1 Arkansas, California, Florida, Illinois, Kentucky, Louisiana, Massachusetts (1 of 2), Missouri, New Mexico, New York (1 of 2), North Carolina, Wisconsin

2 Colorado

beer

3 Hawaii, New York (2 of 2), Pennsylvania (1 of 2)

4 Maine

5 Michigan, Ohio, Pennsylvania (2 of 2), South Carolina, Washington

6 Massachusetts (2 of 2), North Dakota

7 Texas

bird

Not all birds can fly.

1 Alabama

2 Arkansas, California, Colorado, Florida, Illinois, Kentucky, Louisiana, Maine, Massachusetts (1 of 2), Michigan, Missouri, New Mexico, New York, North Carolina, North Dakota, Ohio, Pennsylvania, South Carolina, Texas, Utah, Virginia, Washington, Wisconsin

3 Hawaii, Massachusetts (2 of 2)

birthday

When is your birthday?

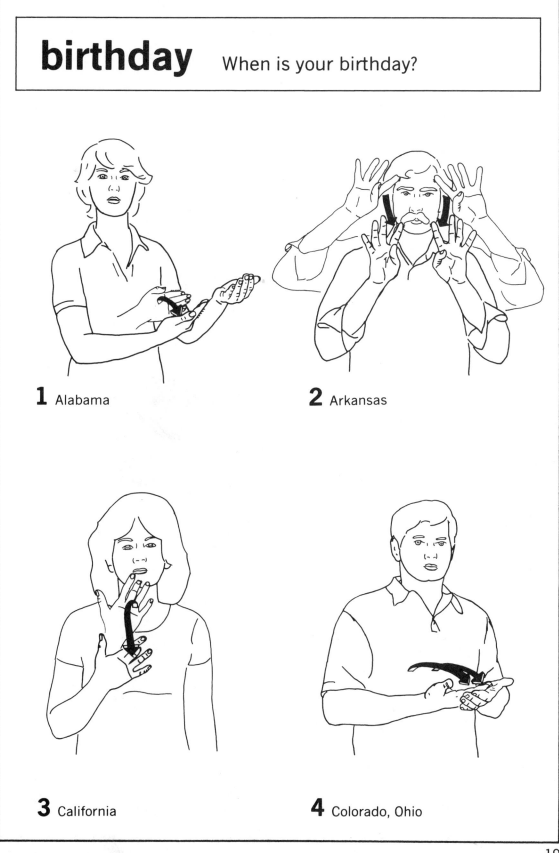

1 Alabama

2 Arkansas

3 California

4 Colorado, Ohio

birthday

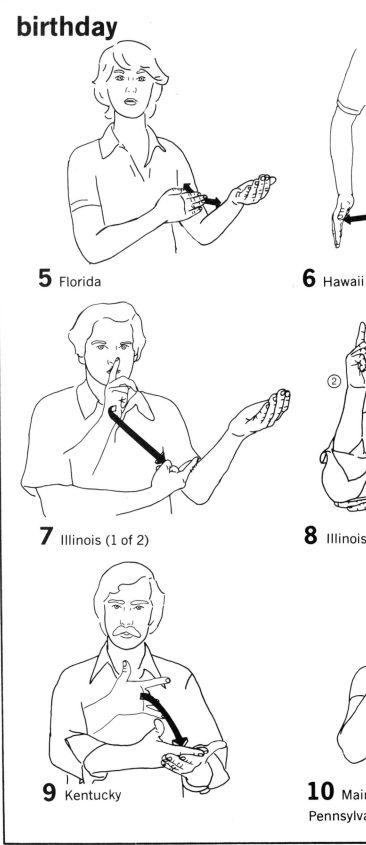

5 Florida

6 Hawaii

7 Illinois (1 of 2)

8 Illinois (2 of 2), Louisiana

9 Kentucky

10 Maine, Massachusetts (1 of 2), Pennsylvania (1 of 2)

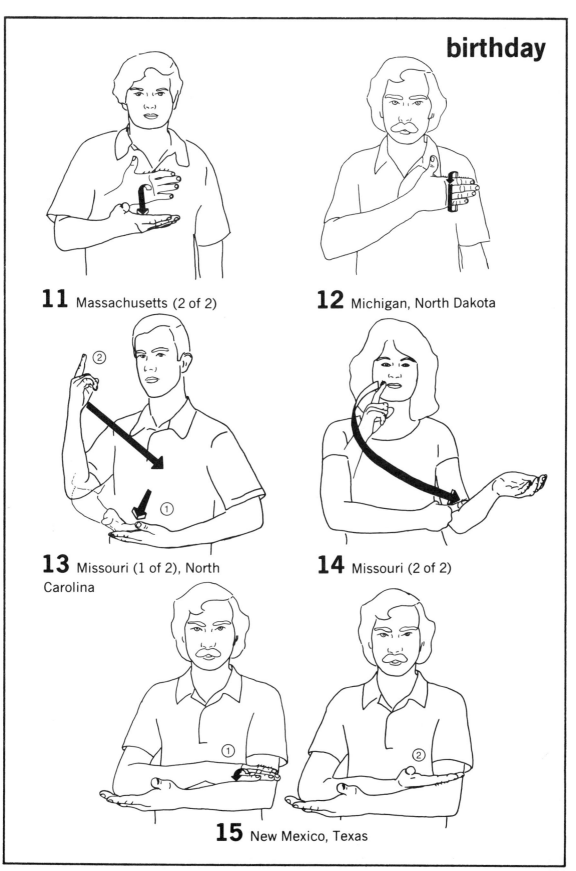

11 Massachusetts (2 of 2)

12 Michigan, North Dakota

13 Missouri (1 of 2), North Carolina

14 Missouri (2 of 2)

15 New Mexico, Texas

birthday

16 New York

17 Pennsylvania (2 of 2)

18 South Carolina

19 Utah

20 Virginia

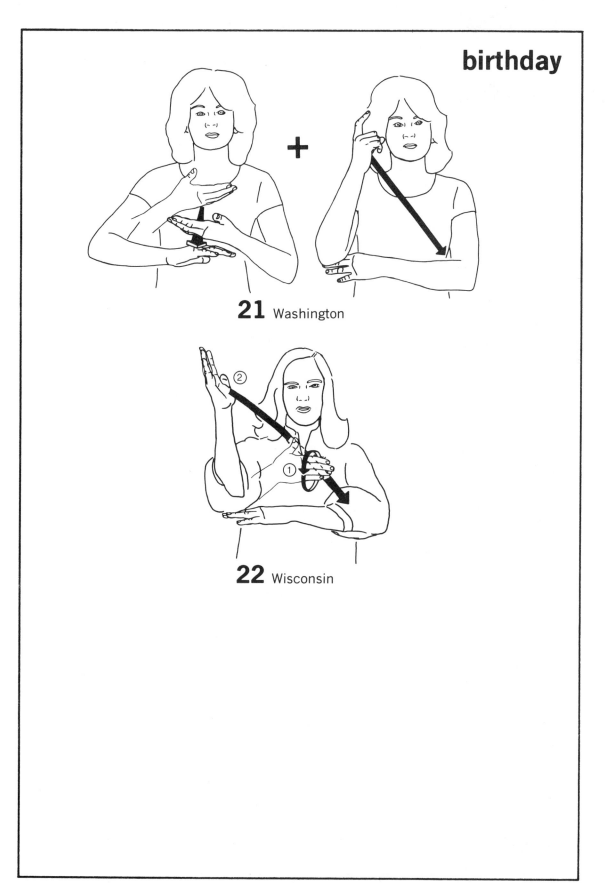

21 Washington

22 Wisconsin

brown

The brown water is full of mud.

1 Alabama

2 Arkansas, Michigan, Ohio

3 California, Colorado

4 Florida, Illinois (1 of 2), Kentucky, New Mexico, New York, North Carolina, Pennsylvania (1 of 3), Texas, Utah, Virginia

brown

5 Hawaii

6 Illinois (2 of 2), Missouri

7 Louisiana, Maine, North Dakota, Pennsylvania (2 of 3), Washington, Wisconsin

8 Massachusetts

9 Pennsylvania (3 of 3)

10 South Carolina

cake

The fudge cake was delicious.

FINGERSPELL: California, Maine

1 Alabama, North Carolina, South Carolina

2 Arkansas (1 of 2), Louisiana

3 Arkansas (2 of 2), Pennsylvania

4 Colorado, Massachusetts, Missouri, Utah, Wisconsin

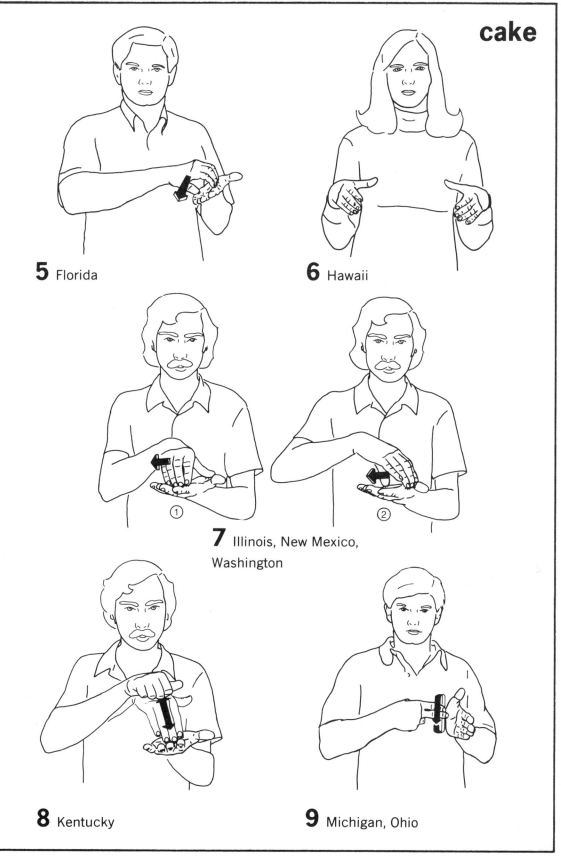

cake

5 Florida

6 Hawaii

7 Illinois, New Mexico, Washington

8 Kentucky

9 Michigan, Ohio

27

cake

10 New York

11 North Dakota

12 Texas

13 Virginia

28

candy

The children ate all their Halloween candy.

1 Alabama, Kentucky, Texas

2 Arkansas, Utah

3 California, Louisiana (1 of 2), Missouri, Washington

4 Colorado

candy

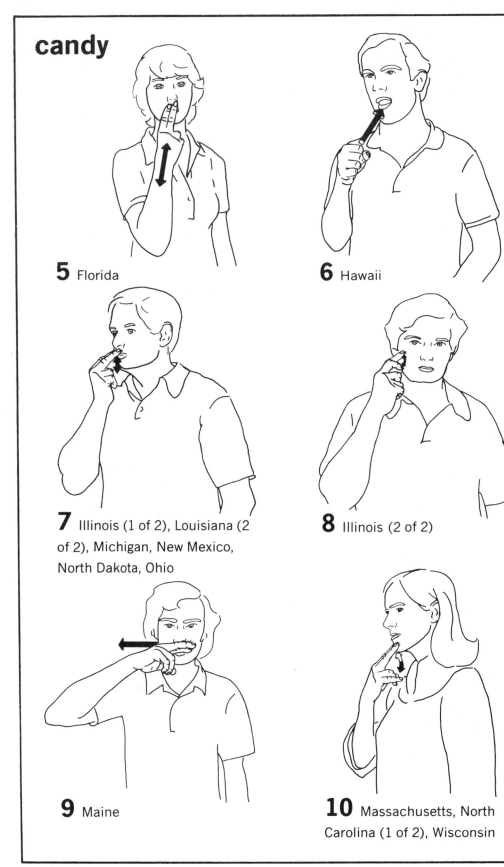

5 Florida

6 Hawaii

7 Illinois (1 of 2), Louisiana (2 of 2), Michigan, New Mexico, North Dakota, Ohio

8 Illinois (2 of 2)

9 Maine

10 Massachusetts, North Carolina (1 of 2), Wisconsin

11 New York, North Carolina
(2 of 2)

12 Pennsylvania

13 South Carolina

14 Virginia

carrot

They planted three rows of carrots.

FINGERSPELL: Alabama, California, Maine, North Dakota, Ohio, South Carolina, Virginia

1 Arkansas

2 Colorado

3 Florida, Kentucky, Louisiana, North Carolina, Utah

4 Hawaii

carrot

5 Illinois

6 Massachusetts

7 Michigan

8 Missouri, Wisconsin

9 New Mexico

10 New York

carrot

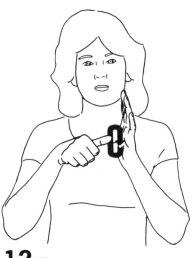

11 Pennsylvania

12 Texas

13 Washington

cat

The cat stalked the bird but never caught it.

1 Alabama (female cat), Arkansas, Colorado

2 Alabama (male cat), Ohio, Texas

3 California, Florida, Illinois, Kentucky, Louisiana, Maine, Massachusetts, Michigan, New Mexico, North Carolina, North Dakota, Pennsylvania, (1 of 2), South Carolina, Virginia, Wisconsin

4 Hawaii, New York, Utah

cat

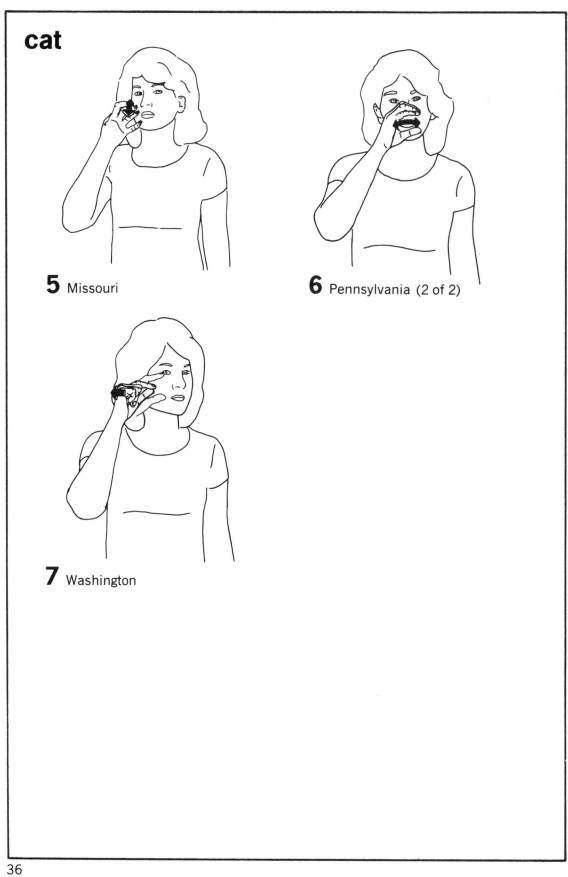

5 Missouri

6 Pennsylvania (2 of 2)

7 Washington

cereal   I eat cereal for breakfast.

FINGERSPELL: Alabama, Hawaii, Maine, Michigan, North Carolina, Texas, Virginia, Wisconsin

1 Arkansas

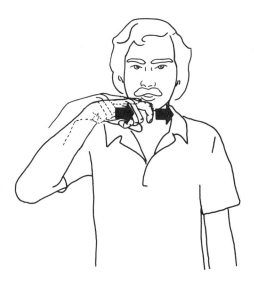

2 California, Kentucky, New Mexico, Utah

3 Colorado

4 Florida, Louisiana

cereal

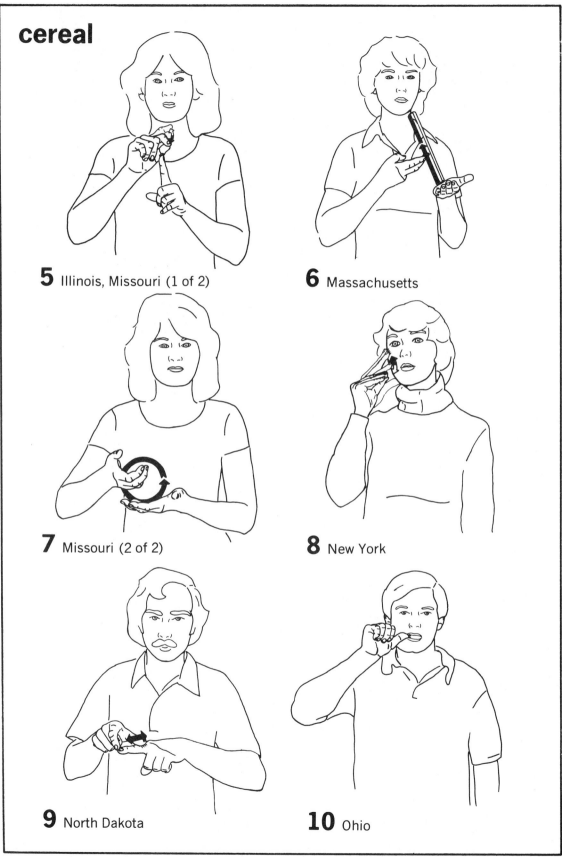

5 Illinois, Missouri (1 of 2)

6 Massachusetts

7 Missouri (2 of 2)

8 New York

9 North Dakota

10 Ohio

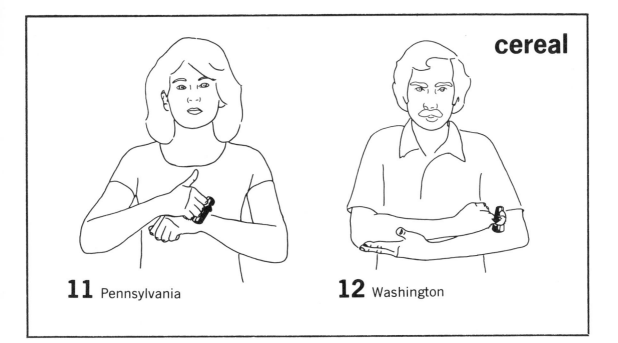

cereal

11 Pennsylvania   **12** Washington

cheat   Did he cheat on the test?

1 Alabama   **2** Arkansas

cheat

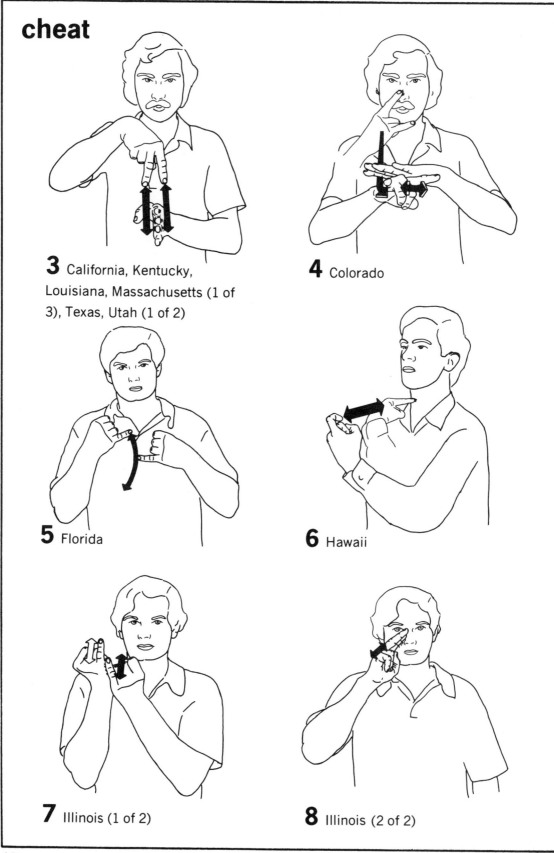

3 California, Kentucky, Louisiana, Massachusetts (1 of 3), Texas, Utah (1 of 2)

4 Colorado

5 Florida

6 Hawaii

7 Illinois (1 of 2)

8 Illinois (2 of 2)

9 Maine

10 Massachusetts (2 of 3)

11 Massachusetts (3 of 3),
Ohio

12 Michigan

13 Missouri

14 New Mexico, Utah (2 of 2),
Wisconsin

cheat

15 New York, Pennsylvania (1 of 2)

16 North Carolina

17 North Dakota

18 Pennsylvania (2 of 2)

19 South Carolina, Virginia

20 Washington

cherry   There is no cherry pie left.

FINGERSPELL: Alabama, Hawaii, North Dakota, South Carolina, Texas

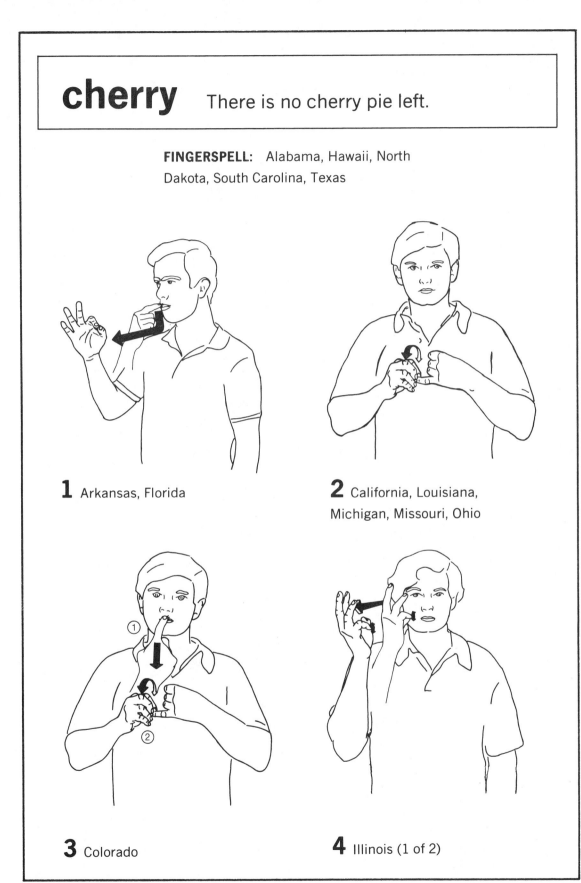

1 Arkansas, Florida

2 California, Louisiana, Michigan, Missouri, Ohio

3 Colorado

4 Illinois (1 of 2)

cherry

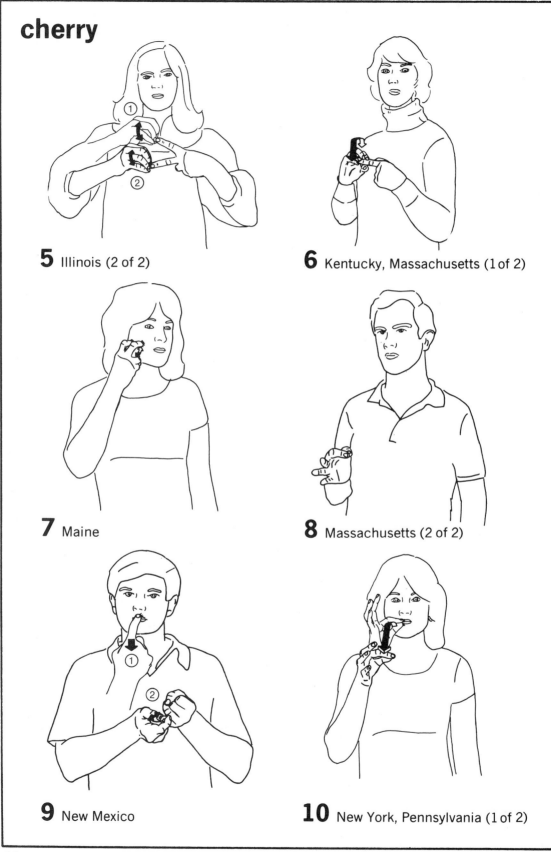

5 Illinois (2 of 2)

6 Kentucky, Massachusetts (1 of 2)

7 Maine

8 Massachusetts (2 of 2)

9 New Mexico

10 New York, Pennsylvania (1 of 2)

11 North Carolina, Virginia

12 Pennsylvania (2 of 2)

13 Utah

14 Washington

15 Wisconsin

chicken

The chicken lays its eggs in the barn.

1 Alabama, Arkansas, California, Colorado, Florida, Kentucky, Maine, Massachussets, Missouri (1 of 2), New York, North Carolina, North Dakota, Pennsylvania (1 of 2), South Carolina, Texas, Virginia

2 Hawaii

3 Illinois (1 of 2)

4 Illinois (2 of 2), Louisiana, Ohio, Washington, Wisconsin

5 Michigan

6 Missouri (2 of 2)

7 New Mexico

8 Pennsylvania (2 of 2), Utah

chocolate

I like chocolate candy.

FINGERSPELL c-h-o-c: Arkansas, Colorado, Missouri

FINGERSPELL: North Carolina, South Carolina

1 Alabama

2 California, Illinois (1 of 2), Kentucky, Massachusetts, New Mexico, Texas, Washington, Wisconsin

3 Florida, Michigan, North Carolina, Ohio

4 Hawaii

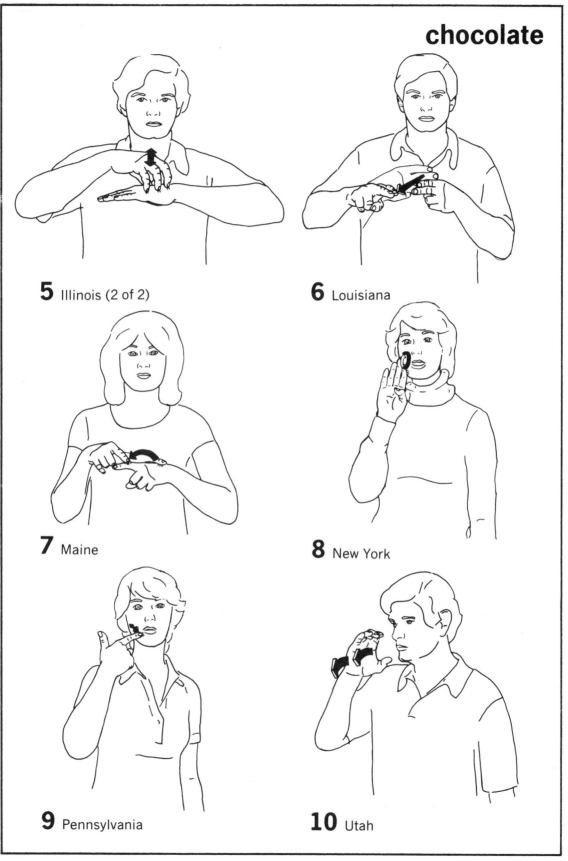

chocolate

5 Illinois (2 of 2)

6 Louisiana

7 Maine

8 New York

9 Pennsylvania

10 Utah

chocolate

11 Virginia

Christmas   Christmas is a joyous time.

1 Alabama, Arkansas, California, Florida, Illinois (1 of 2), Kentucky, Massachusetts (1 of 2), Missouri, New Mexico, New York (1 of 2), North Carolina, Utah, Virginia, Wisconsin

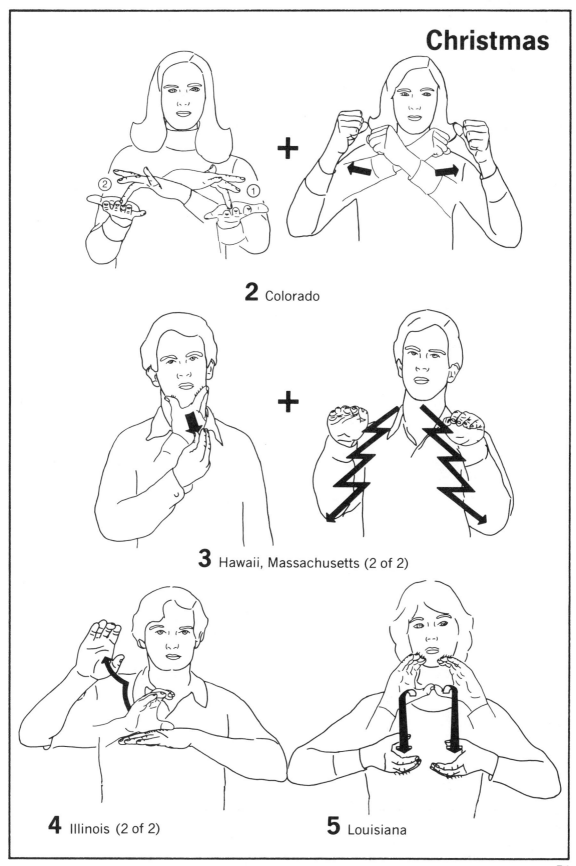

Christmas

2 Colorado

3 Hawaii, Massachusetts (2 of 2)

4 Illinois (2 of 2)

5 Louisiana

51

Christmas

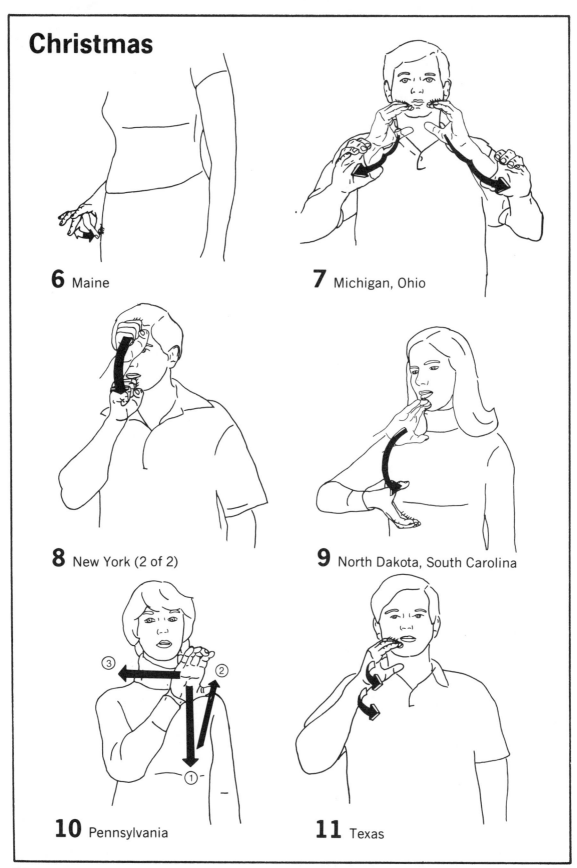

6 Maine

7 Michigan, Ohio

8 New York (2 of 2)

9 North Dakota, South Carolina

10 Pennsylvania

11 Texas

Christmas

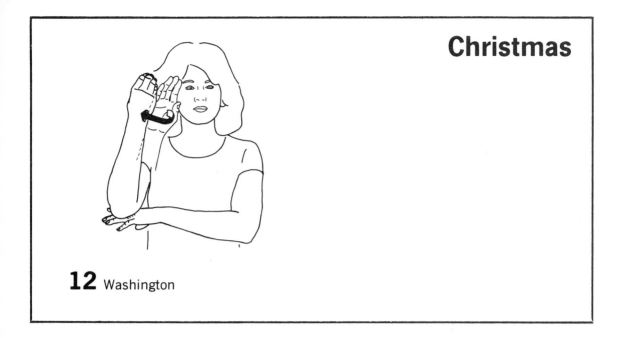

12 Washington

---

circus   The circus is coming next week.

FINGERSPELL: North Carolina, South Carolina, Virginia

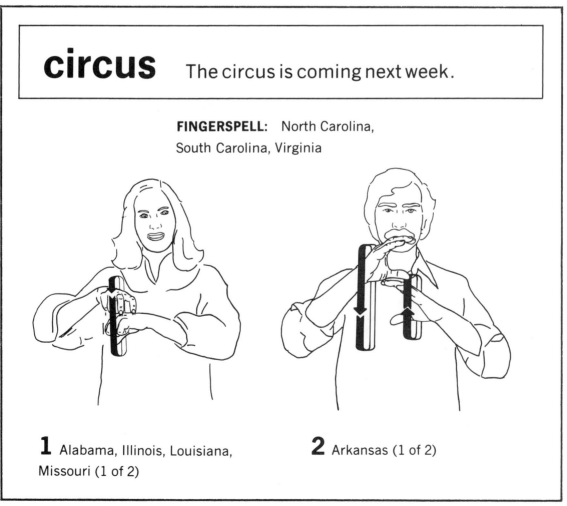

1 Alabama, Illinois, Louisiana, Missouri (1 of 2)

2 Arkansas (1 of 2)

circus

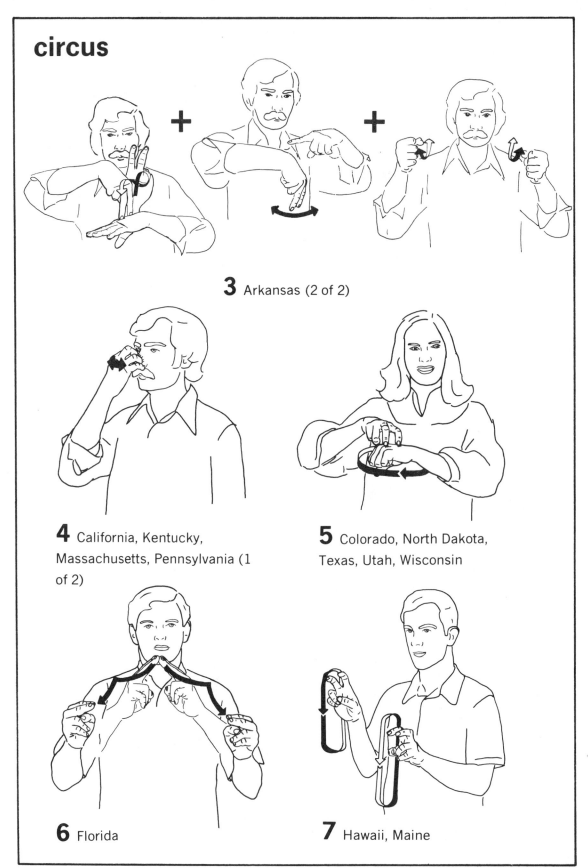

3 Arkansas (2 of 2)

4 California, Kentucky, Massachusetts, Pennsylvania (1 of 2)

5 Colorado, North Dakota, Texas, Utah, Wisconsin

6 Florida

7 Hawaii, Maine

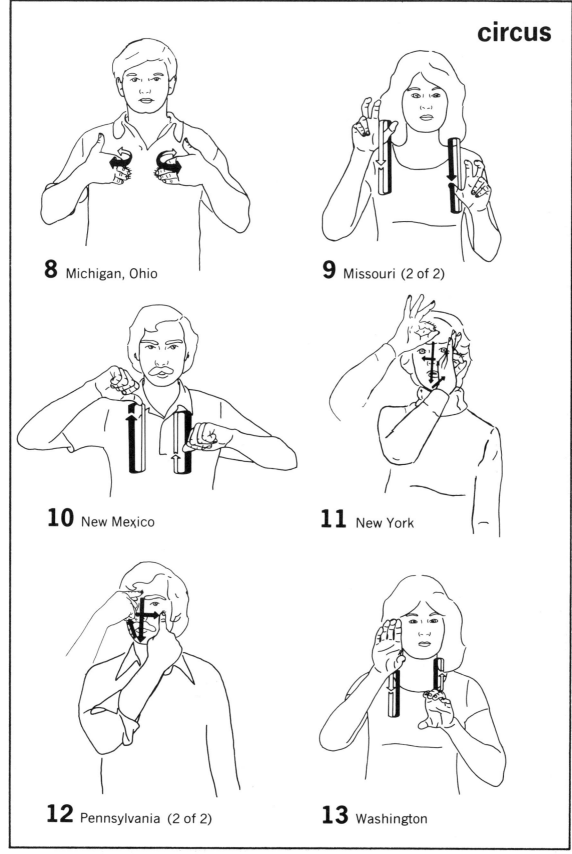

circus

8 Michigan, Ohio

9 Missouri (2 of 2)

10 New Mexico

11 New York

12 Pennsylvania (2 of 2)

13 Washington

clock

My old clock is broken.

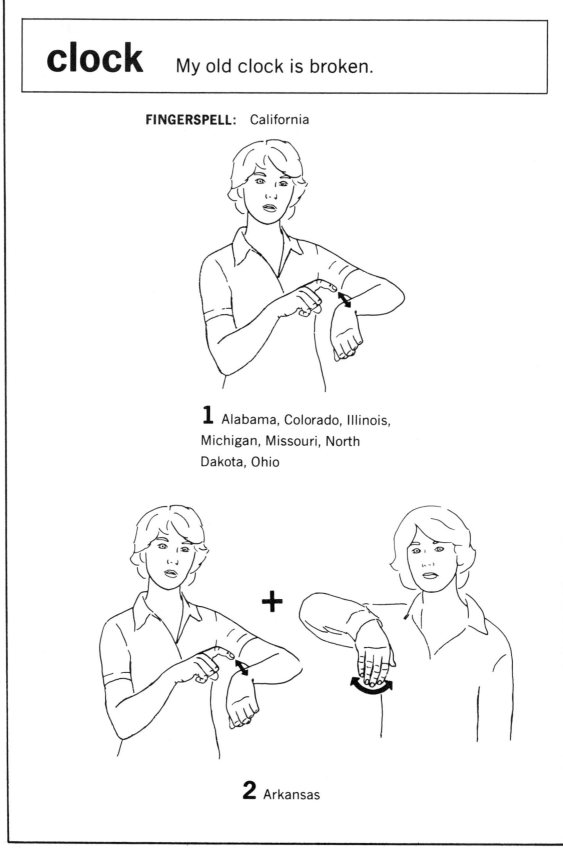

FINGERSPELL: California

1 Alabama, Colorado, Illinois, Michigan, Missouri, North Dakota, Ohio

+

2 Arkansas

clock

3 Florida, Massachusetts (1 of 2)

4 Hawaii, Louisiana, North Carolina, South Carolina, Texas, Virginia

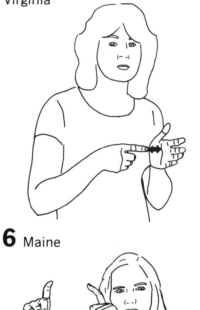

5 Kentucky

6 Maine

7 Massachusetts (2 of 2), Pennsylvania

8 New Mexico, Wisconsin

clock

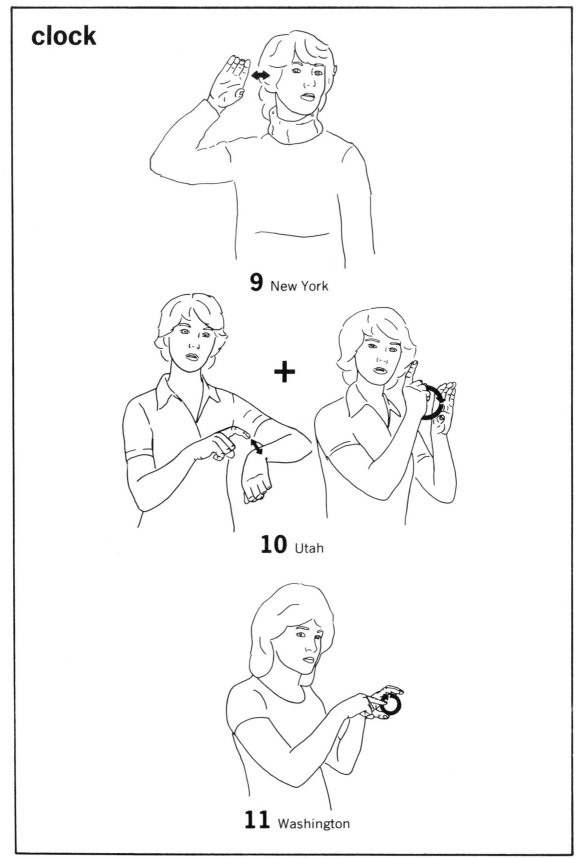

9 New York

+

10 Utah

11 Washington

cookie   The cookies taste awful.

1 Alabama, California, Florida (1 of 2), Illinois, Kentucky, Massachusetts (1 of 2), Missouri, New Mexico, New York, North Carolina, North Dakota, Ohio, Pennsylvania (1 of 2), Utah, Washington

2 Arkansas

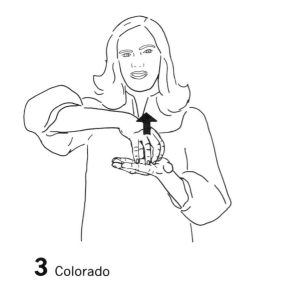

3 Colorado

4 Florida (2 of 2), Louisiana

cookie

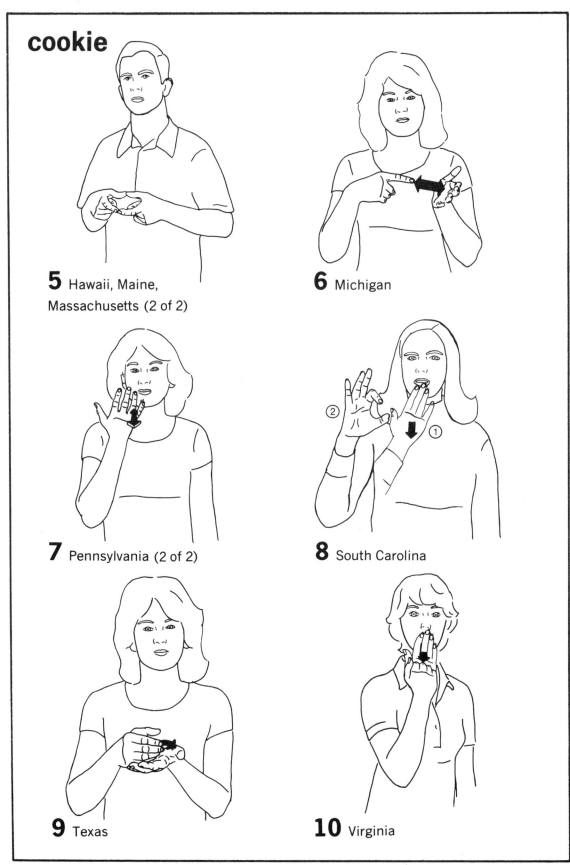

5 Hawaii, Maine, Massachusetts (2 of 2)

6 Michigan

7 Pennsylvania (2 of 2)

8 South Carolina

9 Texas

10 Virginia

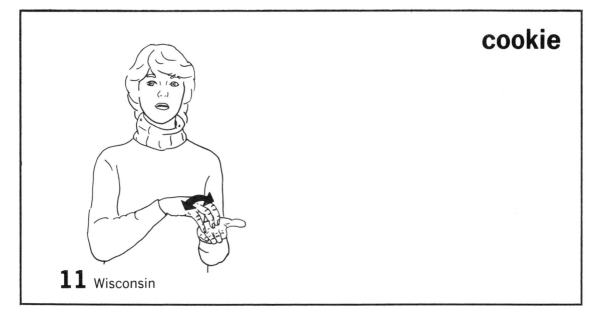

cookie

11 Wisconsin

country

We have a country home and a city home.

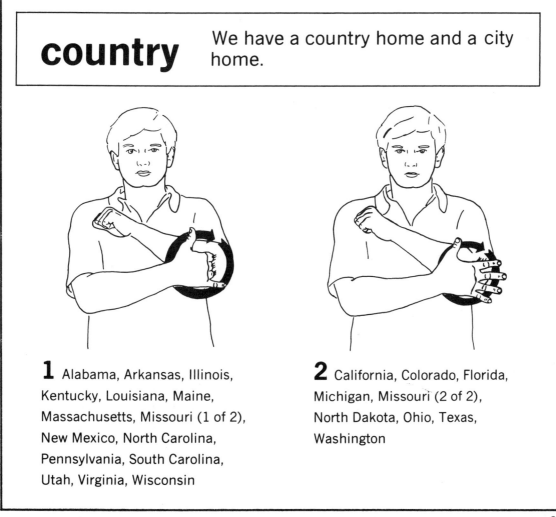

1 Alabama, Arkansas, Illinois, Kentucky, Louisiana, Maine, Massachusetts, Missouri (1 of 2), New Mexico, North Carolina, Pennsylvania, South Carolina, Utah, Virginia, Wisconsin

2 California, Colorado, Florida, Michigan, Missouri (2 of 2), North Dakota, Ohio, Texas, Washington

country

3 Hawaii

4 New York

cracker   At 4:00 we ate crackers and cheese.

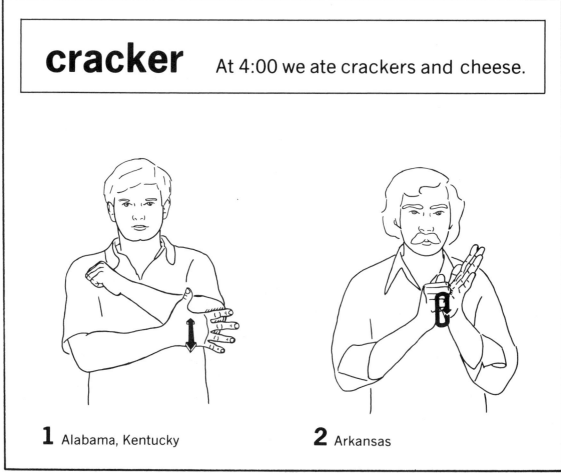

1 Alabama, Kentucky

2 Arkansas

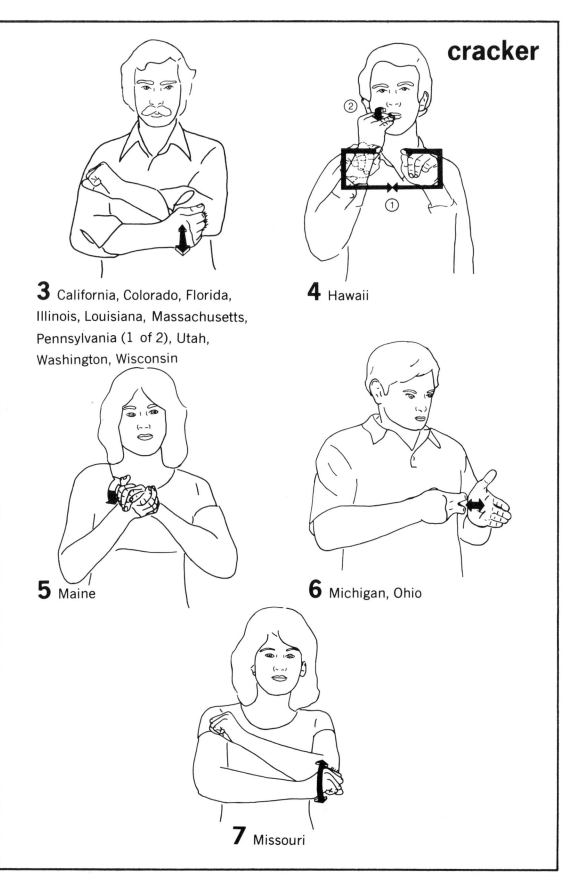

cracker

3 California, Colorado, Florida, Illinois, Louisiana, Massachusetts, Pennsylvania (1 of 2), Utah, Washington, Wisconsin

4 Hawaii

5 Maine

6 Michigan, Ohio

7 Missouri

cracker

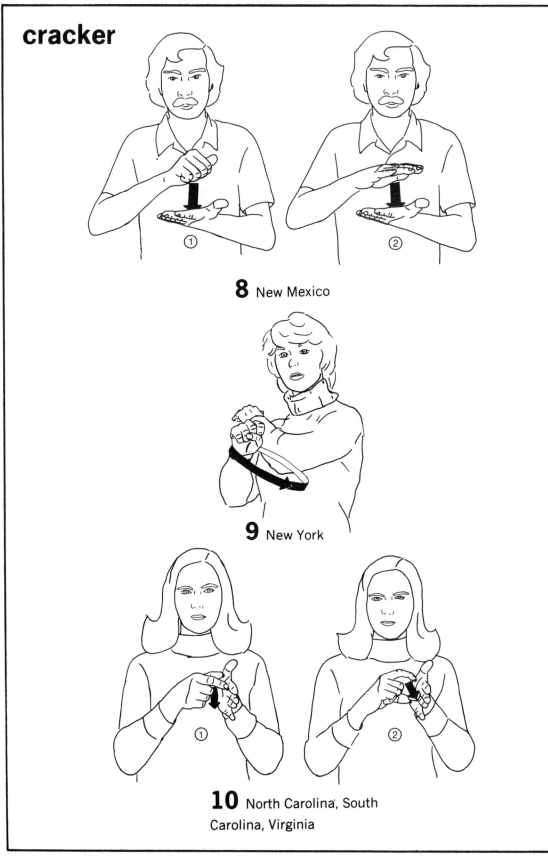

8 New Mexico

9 New York

10 North Carolina, South
Carolina, Virginia

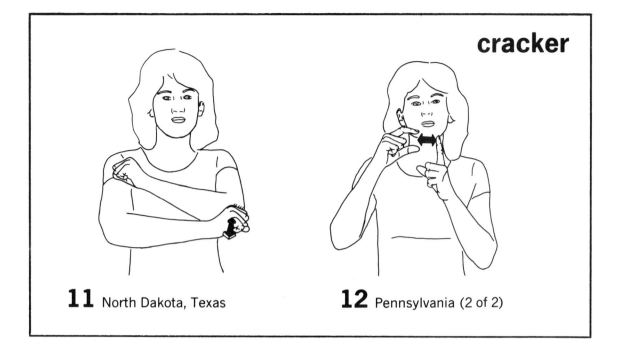

11 North Dakota, Texas

12 Pennsylvania (2 of 2)

delicious Fresh-baked pie tastes delicious.

1 Alabama

2 Arkansas, New Mexico, Utah, Washington

delicious

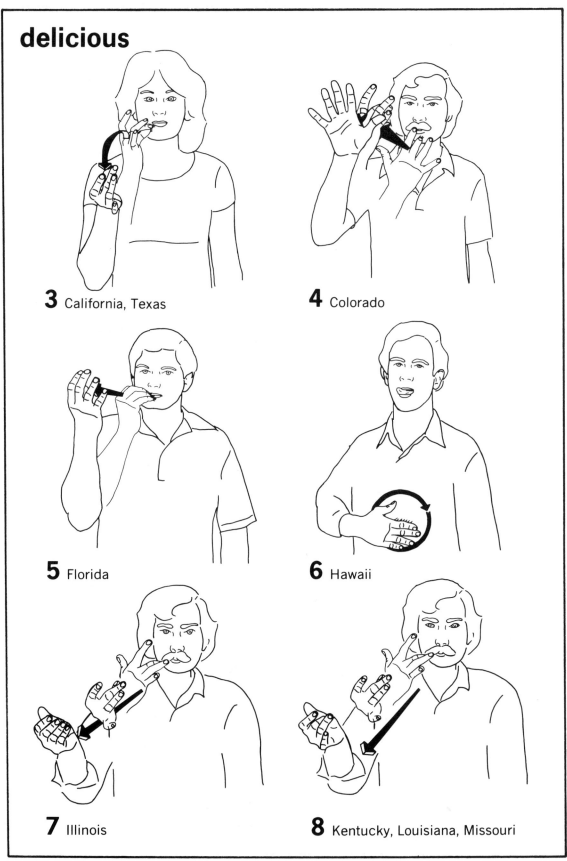

3 California, Texas

4 Colorado

5 Florida

6 Hawaii

7 Illinois

8 Kentucky, Louisiana, Missouri

delicious

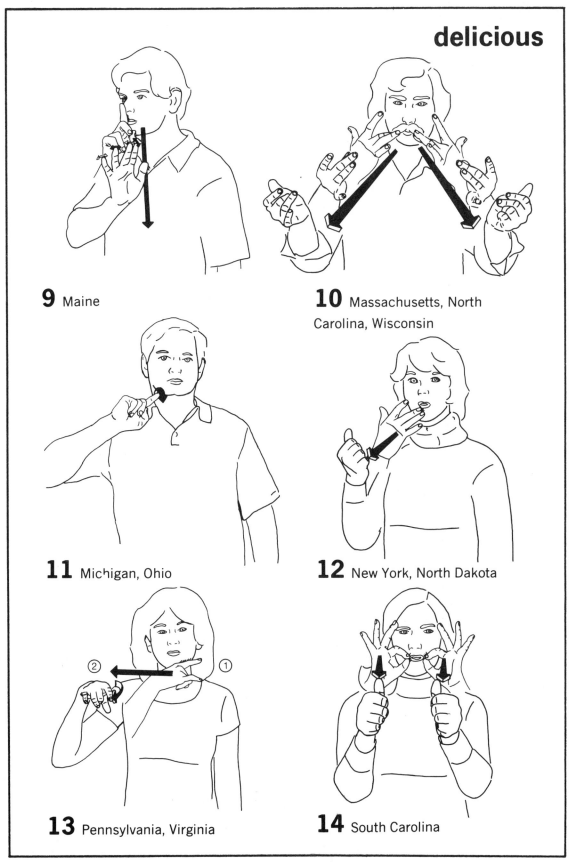

9 Maine

10 Massachusetts, North Carolina, Wisconsin

11 Michigan, Ohio

12 New York, North Dakota

13 Pennsylvania, Virginia

14 South Carolina

dog   The dog barked at the cat.

FINGERSPELL: California, Wisconsin

1 Alabama, Kentucky, Massachusetts, Missouri, North Carolina, South Carolina, Texas, Virginia

2 Arkansas, Colorado, Florida, Illinois (1 of 2), Louisiana, New Mexico, Ohio, Pennsylvania (1 of 2), Utah, Washington

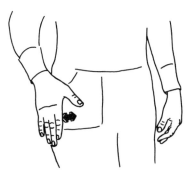

3 Hawaii

4 Illinois (2 of 2), Maine, Michigan, North Dakota

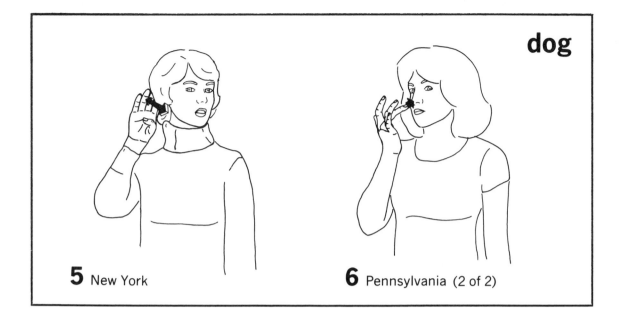

dog

5 New York

6 Pennsylvania (2 of 2)

doll Tracy wants a new doll.

1 Alabama, Arkansas, California, Colorado, Florida, Illinois, Kentucky, Louisiana, Massachusetts, Missouri, New Mexico, North Carolina, South Carolina, Texas, Utah, Virginia, Washington

2 Hawaii

doll

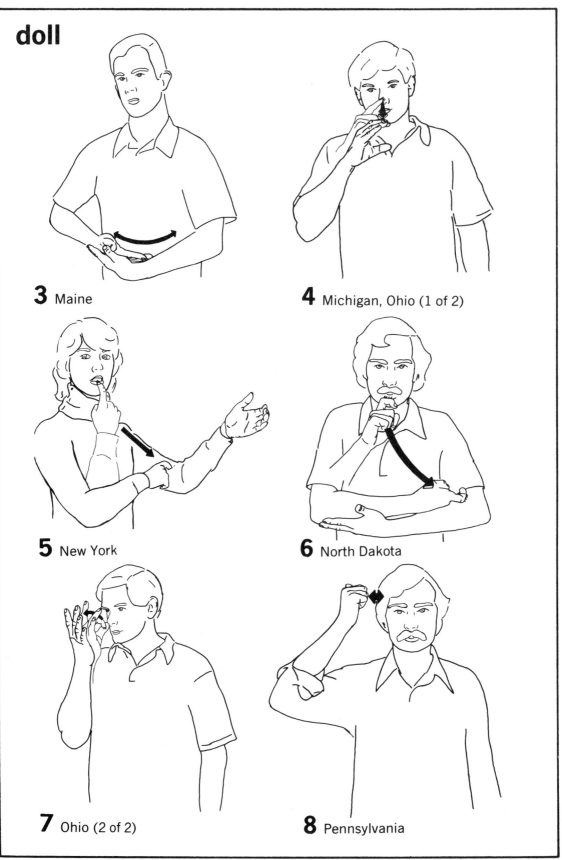

3 Maine

4 Michigan, Ohio (1 of 2)

5 New York

6 North Dakota

7 Ohio (2 of 2)

8 Pennsylvania

doll

9 Wisconsin

---

early   Be sure to get to the station early.

FINGERSPELL: Ohio, Pennsylvania

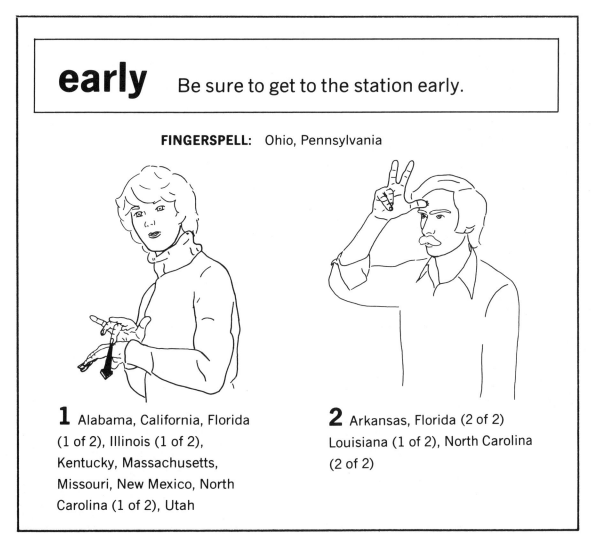

1 Alabama, California, Florida
(1 of 2), Illinois (1 of 2),
Kentucky, Massachusetts,
Missouri, New Mexico, North
Carolina (1 of 2), Utah

2 Arkansas, Florida (2 of 2)
Louisiana (1 of 2), North Carolina
(2 of 2)

early

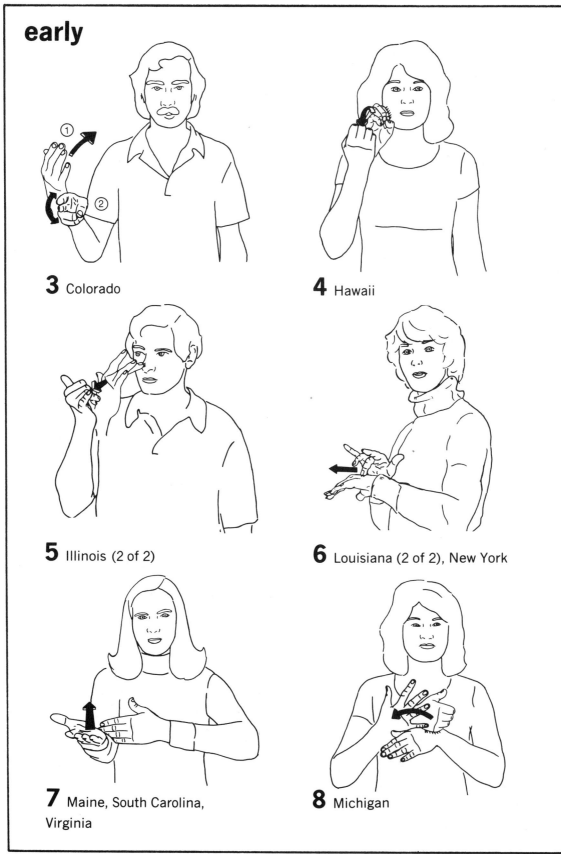

3 Colorado

4 Hawaii

5 Illinois (2 of 2)

6 Louisiana (2 of 2), New York

7 Maine, South Carolina, Virginia

8 Michigan

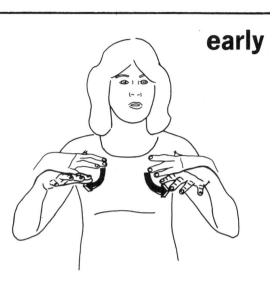

9 North Dakota

10 Texas

11 Washington

12 Wisconsin

Easter

Easter is always on Sunday.

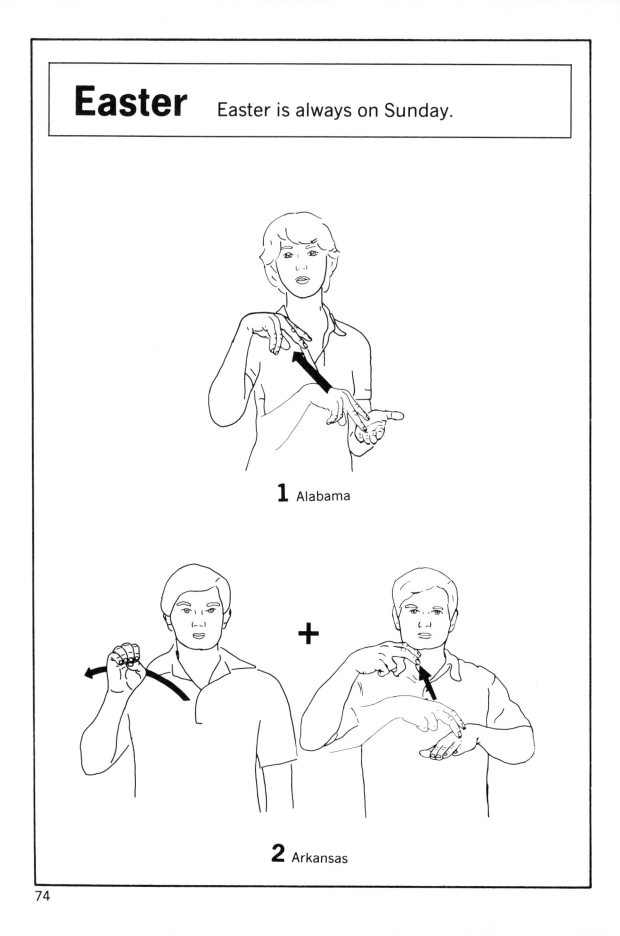

1 Alabama

2 Arkansas

3 California, Missouri (1 of 2), New York, North Carolina, Pennsylvania (1 of 4), Texas

4 Colorado, Michigan, Ohio, Pennsylvania (2 of 4)

5 Florida, Illinois, Kentucky, Louisiana, Massachusetts, New Mexico, Washington, Wisconsin

6 Hawaii

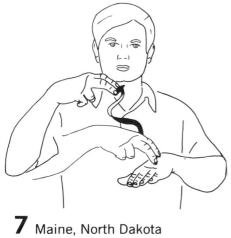

7 Maine, North Dakota

8 Missouri (2 of 2)

Easter

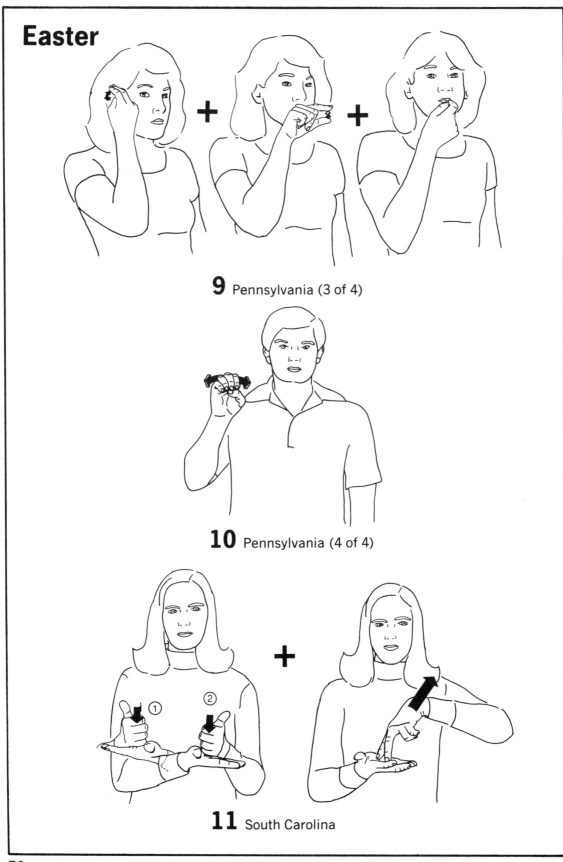

9 Pennsylvania (3 of 4)

10 Pennsylvania (4 of 4)

11 South Carolina

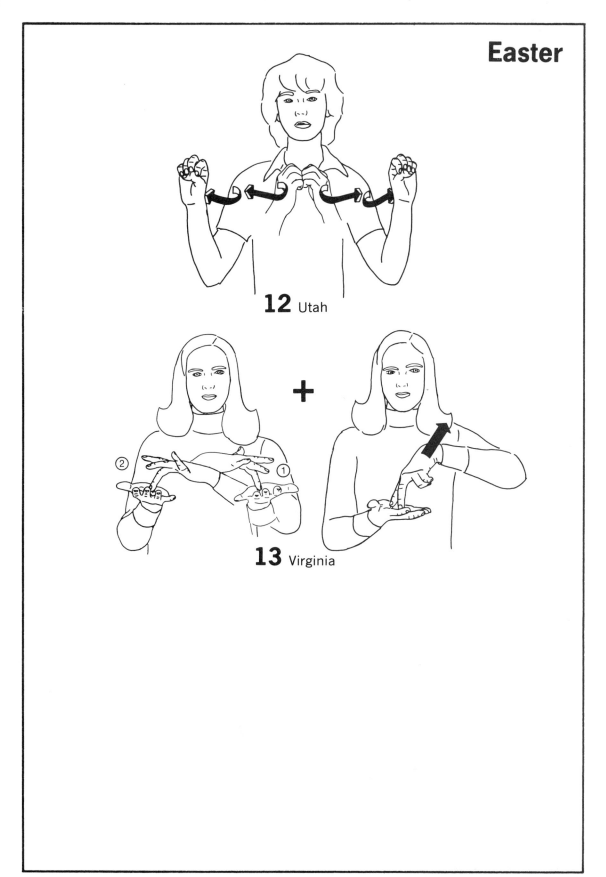

Easter

12 Utah

+

13 Virginia

faint

My mother fainted from the ammonia fumes.

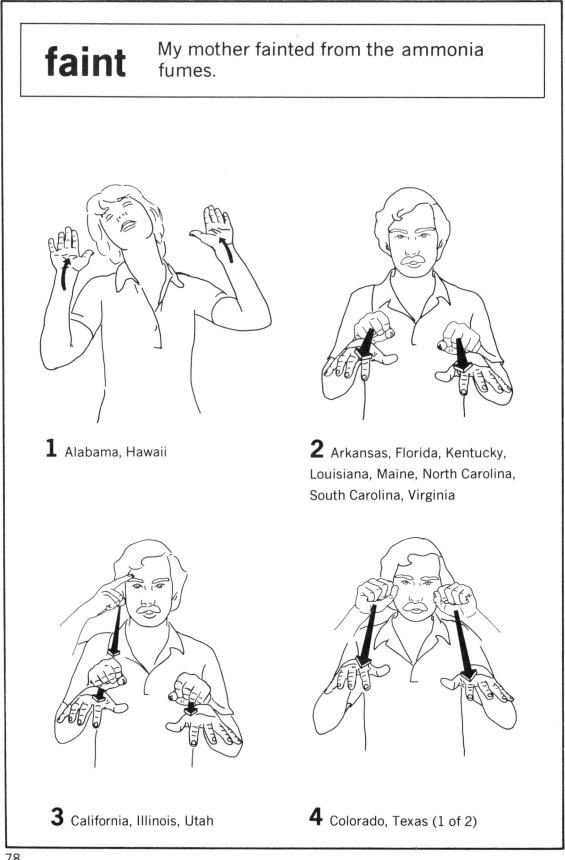

1 Alabama, Hawaii

2 Arkansas, Florida, Kentucky, Louisiana, Maine, North Carolina, South Carolina, Virginia

3 California, Illinois, Utah

4 Colorado, Texas (1 of 2)

5 Massachusetts

6 Michigan, Ohio

7 Missouri, New Mexico, Washington

8 New York

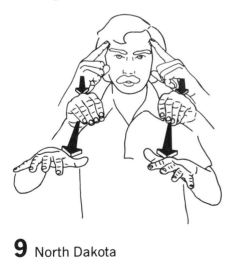

9 North Dakota

10 Pennsylvania

faint

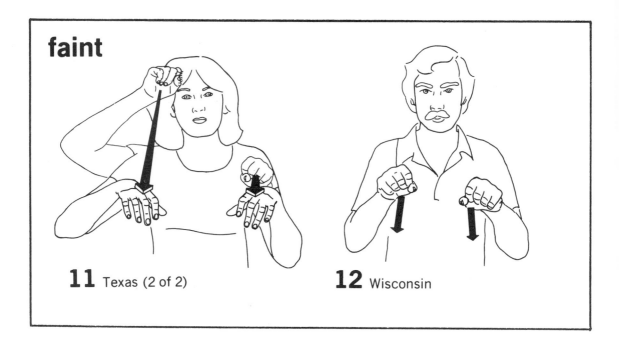

11 Texas (2 of 2) **12** Wisconsin

fair Her artwork is only fair.

FINGERSPELL: North Carolina, South Carolina

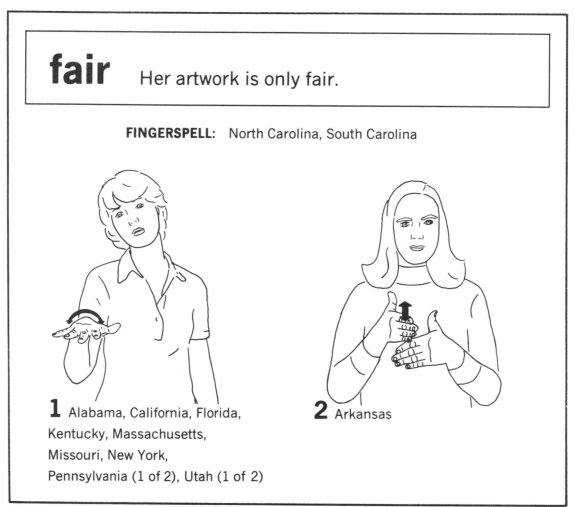

1 Alabama, California, Florida,
Kentucky, Massachusetts,
Missouri, New York,
Pennsylvania (1 of 2), Utah (1 of 2)

2 Arkansas

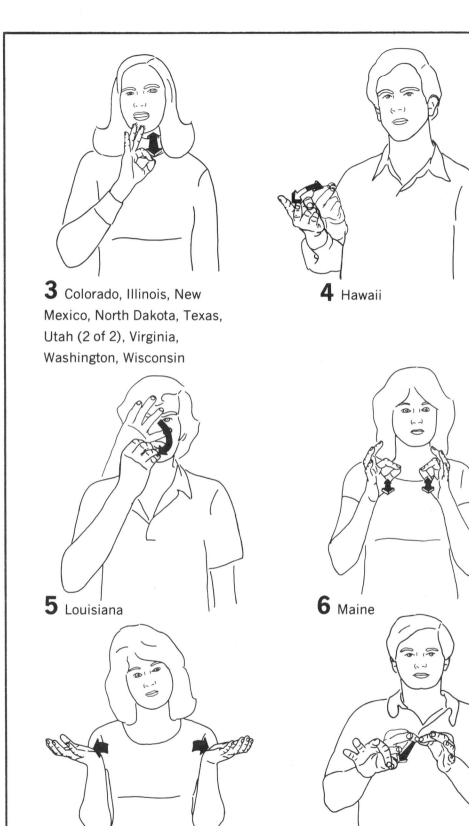

3 Colorado, Illinois, New Mexico, North Dakota, Texas, Utah (2 of 2), Virginia, Washington, Wisconsin

4 Hawaii

5 Louisiana

6 Maine

7 Michigan

8 Ohio

fair

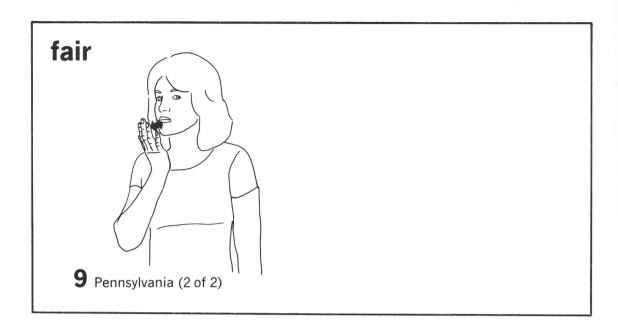

9 Pennsylvania (2 of 2)

fake
The man gave a fake $10 bill to the cashier.

1 Alabama, California, Colorado, Florida, Kentucky, Louisiana, Massachusetts, Missouri (1 of 2), New Mexico, Utah, Washington, Wisconsin

2 Arkansas, Maine, North Carolina, South Carolina, Virginia

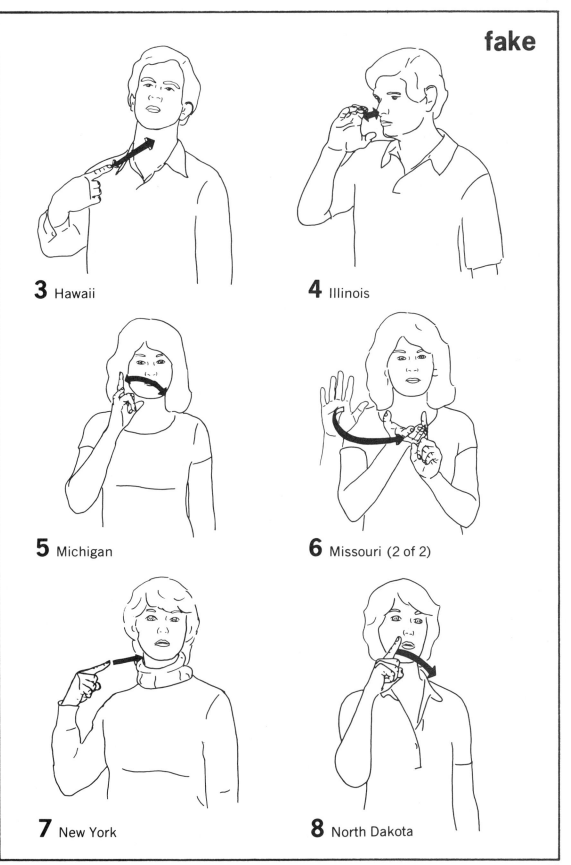

3 Hawaii

4 Illinois

5 Michigan

6 Missouri (2 of 2)

7 New York

8 North Dakota

fake

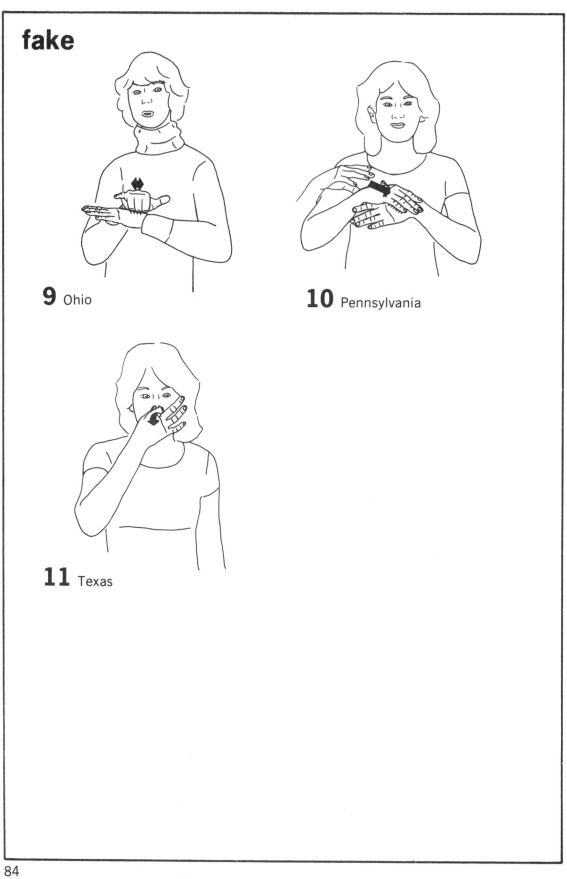

9 Ohio

10 Pennsylvania

11 Texas

fast   He can run fast.

1 Alabama, Florida, Illinois (1 of 2), Kentucky, Louisiana, Missouri, North Carolina, Utah (1 of 2), Virginia, Washington

2 Arkansas, California, Illinois (2 of 2), Maine, Massachusetts, New Mexico, Utah (2 of 2), Wisconsin

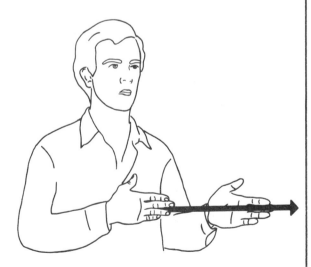

3 Colorado, Michigan, North Dakota, Ohio, South Carolina, Texas

4 Hawaii

fast

5 New York

6 Pennsylvania

favorite   Pecan pie is her favorite dessert.

FINGERSPELL: Alabama, Colorado,
FINGERSPELL f-a-v: Michigan

1 Arkansas, California, Florida,
Illinois (1 of 2), Kentucky,
Louisiana, Maine, Massachusetts
(1 of 2), North Carolina,
Pennsylvania (1 of 3), South
Carolina, Utah, Virginia

2 Hawaii

3 Illinois (2 of 2), Washington

4 Massachusetts (2 of 2), Pennsylvania (2 of 3)

5 Missouri

6 New Mexico

7 New York

8 North Dakota

favorite

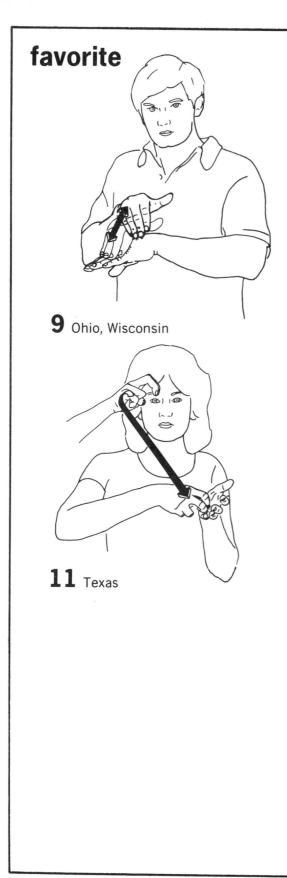

9 Ohio, Wisconsin

10 Pennsylvania (3 of 3)

11 Texas

fire The fire destroyed the warehouse.

1 Alabama

2 Arkansas

3 California, Colorado, Florida, Hawaii, Louisiana, Maine, Pennsylvania (1 of 2), Utah (1 of 2), Virginia

4 Illinois, Missouri, New Mexico, North Carolina, North Dakota, Utah (2 of 2), Washington, Wisconsin

fire

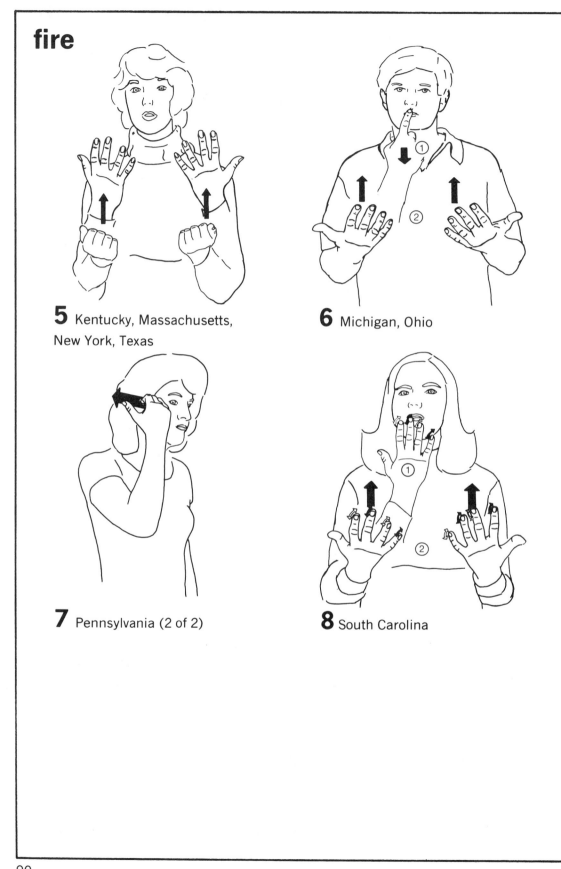

5 Kentucky, Massachusetts, New York, Texas

6 Michigan, Ohio

7 Pennsylvania (2 of 2)

8 South Carolina

fix

I can't fix the toaster.

FINGERSPELL: California, Illinois, Wisconsin

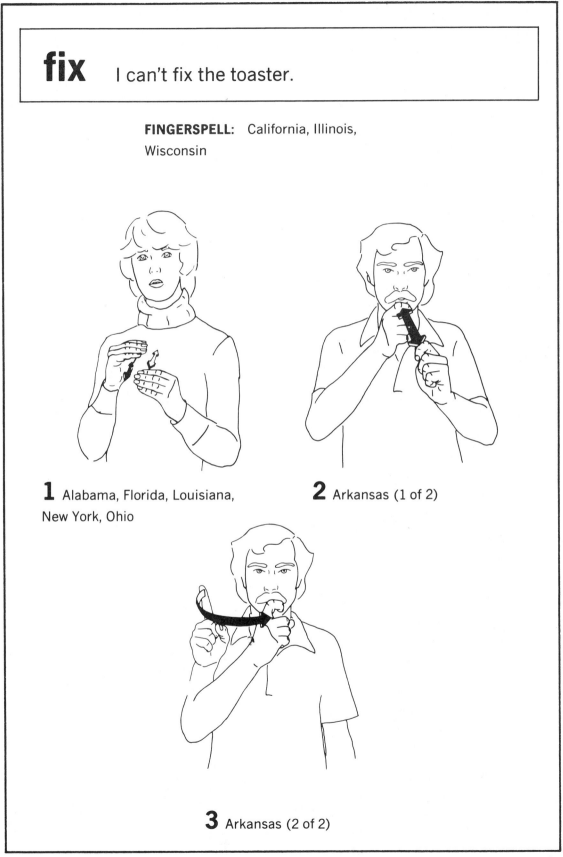

1 Alabama, Florida, Louisiana, New York, Ohio

2 Arkansas (1 of 2)

3 Arkansas (2 of 2)

fix

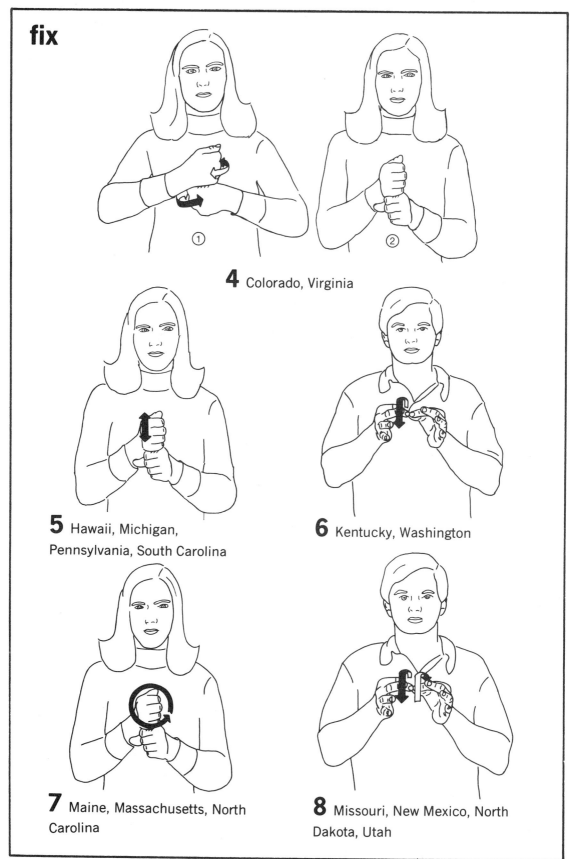

4 Colorado, Virginia

5 Hawaii, Michigan,
Pennsylvania, South Carolina

6 Kentucky, Washington

7 Maine, Massachusetts, North
Carolina

8 Missouri, New Mexico, North
Dakota, Utah

92

fix

9 Texts

flower   The flowers look beautiful in that vase.

① ②

1 Alabama, Ohio, Texas

flower

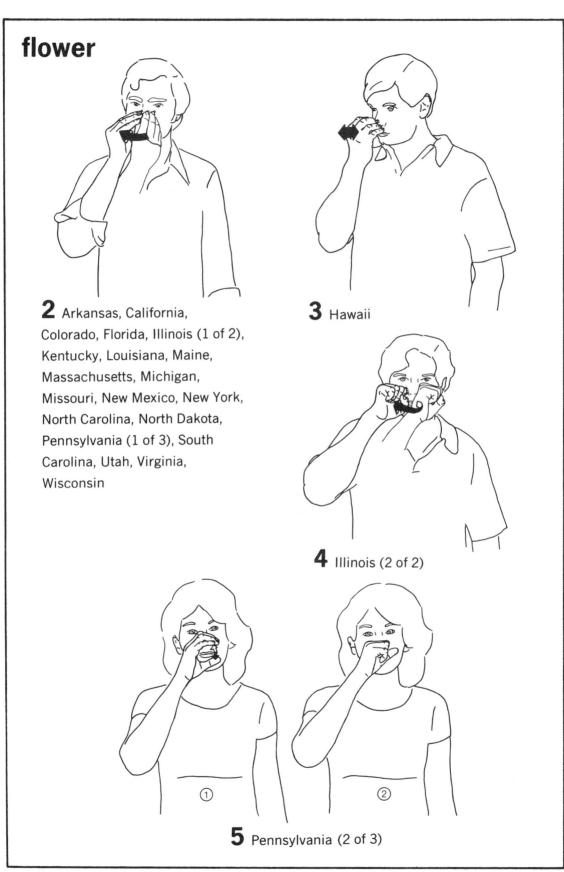

2 Arkansas, California, Colorado, Florida, Illinois (1 of 2), Kentucky, Louisiana, Maine, Massachusetts, Michigan, Missouri, New Mexico, New York, North Carolina, North Dakota, Pennsylvania (1 of 3), South Carolina, Utah, Virginia, Wisconsin

3 Hawaii

4 Illinois (2 of 2)

① ②

5 Pennsylvania (2 of 3)

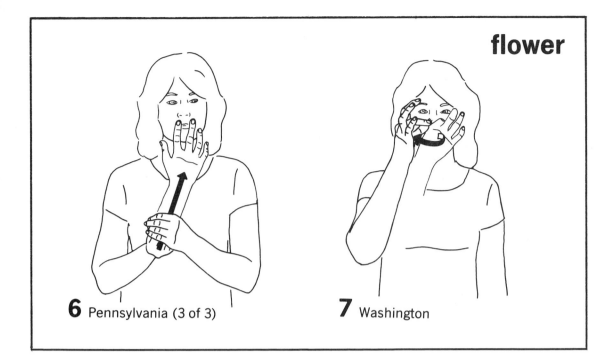

flower

6 Pennsylvania (3 of 3)

7 Washington

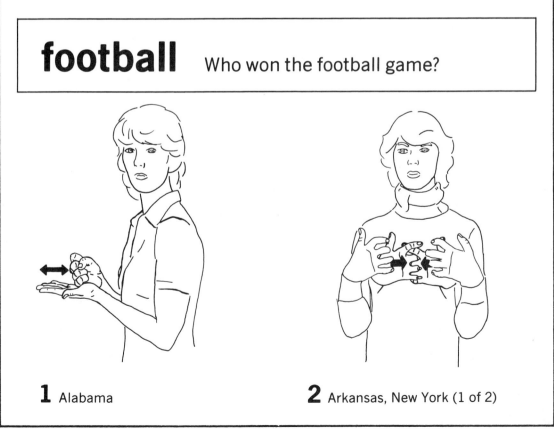

football   Who won the football game?

1 Alabama

2 Arkansas, New York (1 of 2)

football

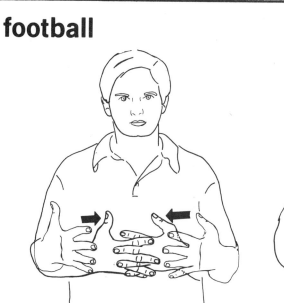

3 California, Florida (1 of 2), Kentucky, Louisiana, Massachusetts, Michigan, Missouri, New Mexico, North Carolina, North Dakota, Ohio (1 of 2), Pennsylvania (1 of 5), Washington

4 Colorado, Illinois (1 of 2), Pennsylvania (2 of 5), South Carolina, Texas, Utah, Virginia, Wisconsin

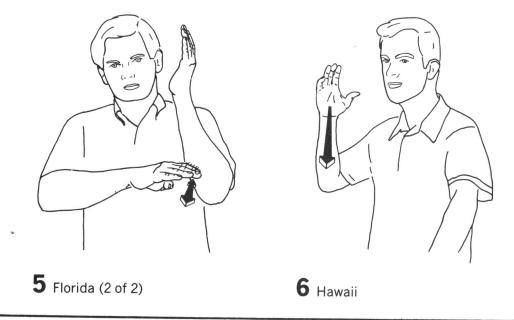

5 Florida (2 of 2)

6 Hawaii

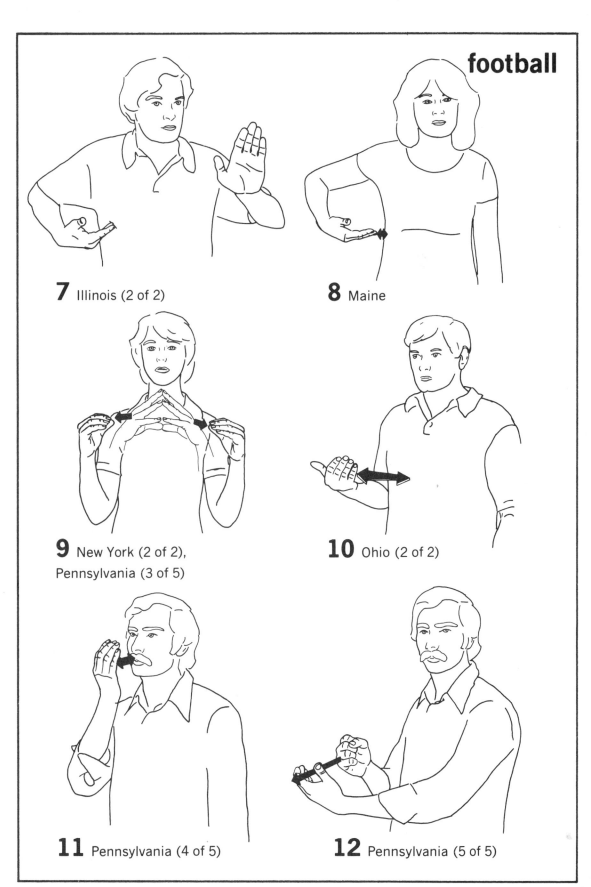

7 Illinois (2 of 2)

8 Maine

9 New York (2 of 2),
Pennsylvania (3 of 5)

10 Ohio (2 of 2)

11 Pennsylvania (4 of 5)

12 Pennsylvania (5 of 5)

Friday

Friday is the busiest day at the shop.

1 Alabama, Arkansas, California, Colorado, Florida, Illinois, Kentucky, Louisiana, Maine, Massachusetts, Michigan, Missouri, New Mexico, New York, North Carolina (1 of 2), North Dakota, Ohio, Pennsylvania, South Carolina, Texas, Utah, Virginia, Washington, Wisconsin

2 Hawaii

3 North Carolina (2 of 2)

game   The game was tied at halftime.

FINGERSPELL: Alabama, Colorado, Maine

1 Arkansas, California, Florida,
Hawaii, Illinois, Kentucky,
Louisiana, Massachusetts,
Michigan, Missouri, New Mexico,
North Carolina, North Dakota,
Pennsylvania, South Carolina,
Texas, Utah, Virginia,
Washington, Wisconsin

2 New York

3 Ohio

gift

We received many anniversary gifts.

FINGERSPELL: Colorado

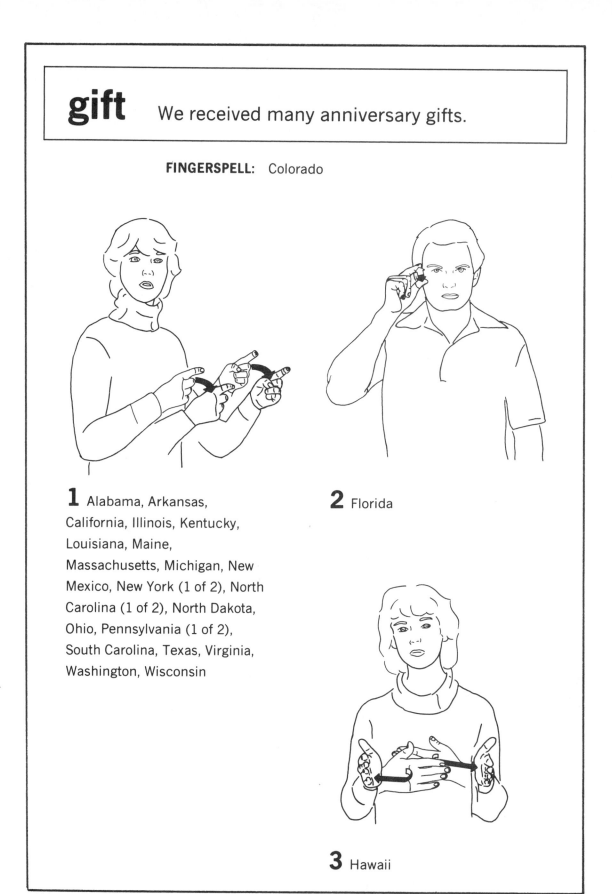

1 Alabama, Arkansas, California, Illinois, Kentucky, Louisiana, Maine, Massachusetts, Michigan, New Mexico, New York (1 of 2), North Carolina (1 of 2), North Dakota, Ohio, Pennsylvania (1 of 2), South Carolina, Texas, Virginia, Washington, Wisconsin

2 Florida

3 Hawaii

4 Missouri

5 New York (2 of 2)

6 North Carolina (2 of 2)

7 Pennsylvania (2 of 2)

+

8 Utah

grapes

The grapes are green.

FINGERSPELL: California, Florida, Illinois, New Mexico, Virginia

1 Alabama

2 Arkansas, Colorado, Kentucky, Louisiana, Michigan, Missouri, New York, North Dakota, Ohio, Pennsylvania (1 of 2), Texas, Utah, Washington, Wisconsin

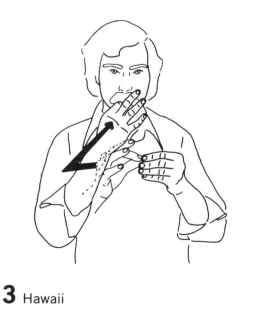

3 Hawaii

4 Maine, North Carolina

102

5 Massachusetts

6 Pennsylvania (2 of 2)

7 South Carolina

gravy

Put the gravy on the table.

1 Alabama, North Carolina, South Carolina, Virginia

2 Arkansas, Florida, Illinois, Kentucky, Louisiana, New Mexico, New York, Pennsylvania (1 of 2), Texas, Washington, Wisconsin

3 California, Michigan, North Dakota, Ohio

4 Colorado

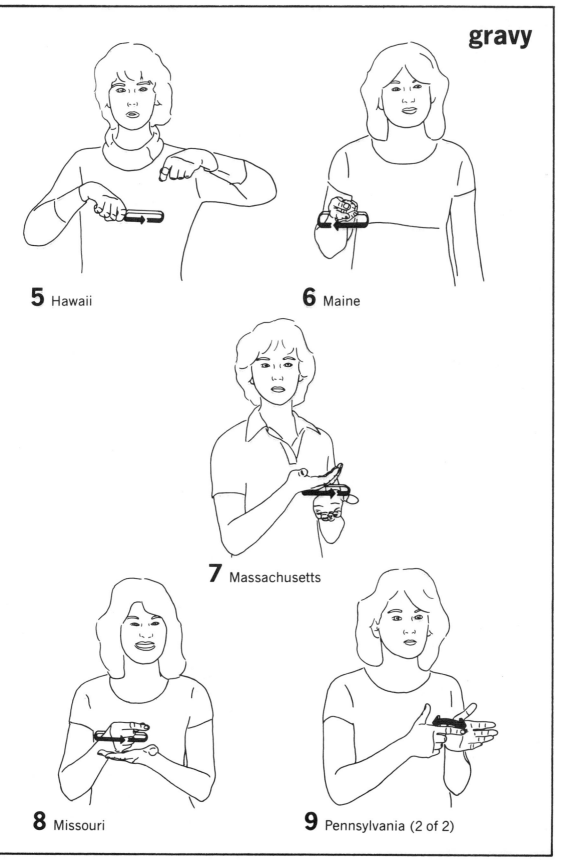

5 Hawaii

6 Maine

7 Massachusetts

8 Missouri

9 Pennsylvania (2 of 2)

gravy

10 Utah

grey · The grey house on the corner is for sale.

FINGERSPELL: Arkansas, Maine, South Carolina, Texas, Virginia

1 Alabama

2 California, Colorado, Louisiana, Massachusetts, New Mexico, North Carolina, Utah

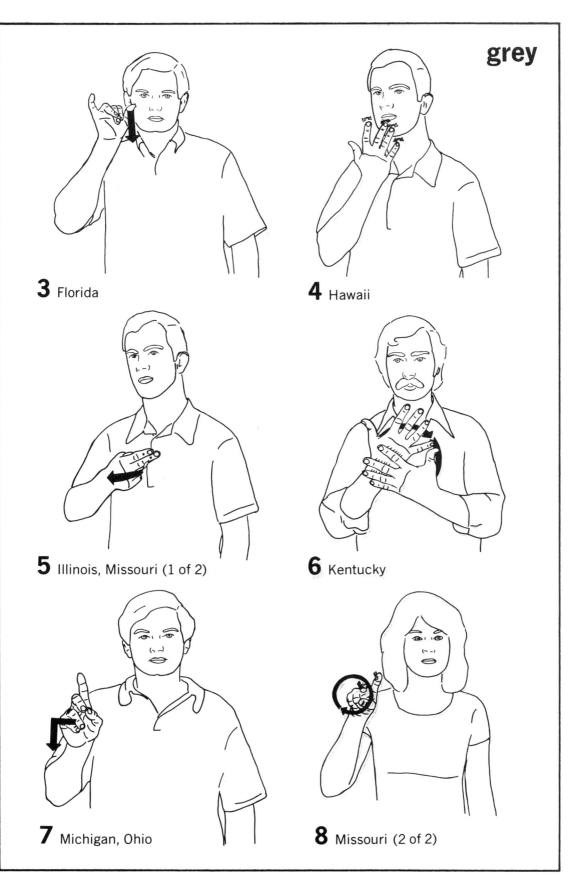

3 Florida

4 Hawaii

5 Illinois, Missouri (1 of 2)

6 Kentucky

7 Michigan, Ohio

8 Missouri (2 of 2)

grey

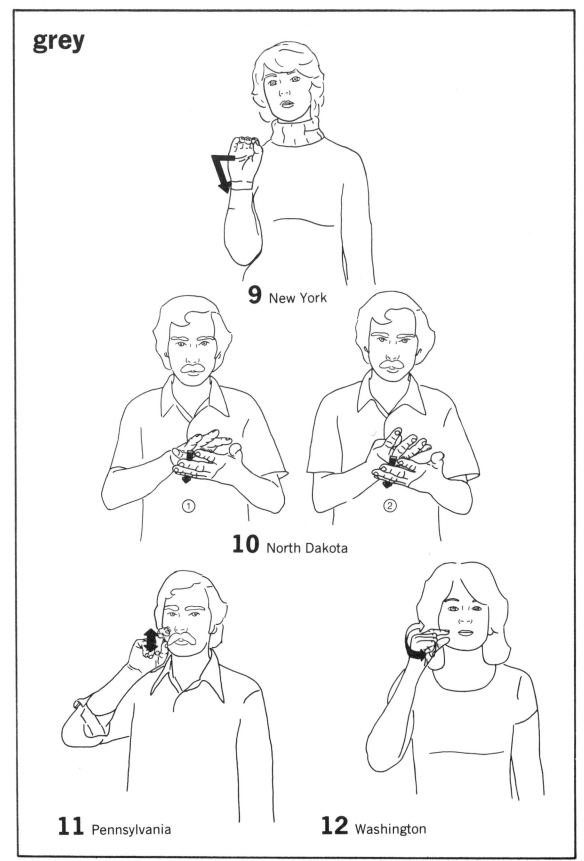

9 New York

10 North Dakota

①   ②

11 Pennsylvania   **12** Washington

13 Wisconsin

Halloween

She made a costume for the Halloween party.

FINGERSPELL: New Mexico, South Carolina

1 Alabama

2 Arkansas

Halloween

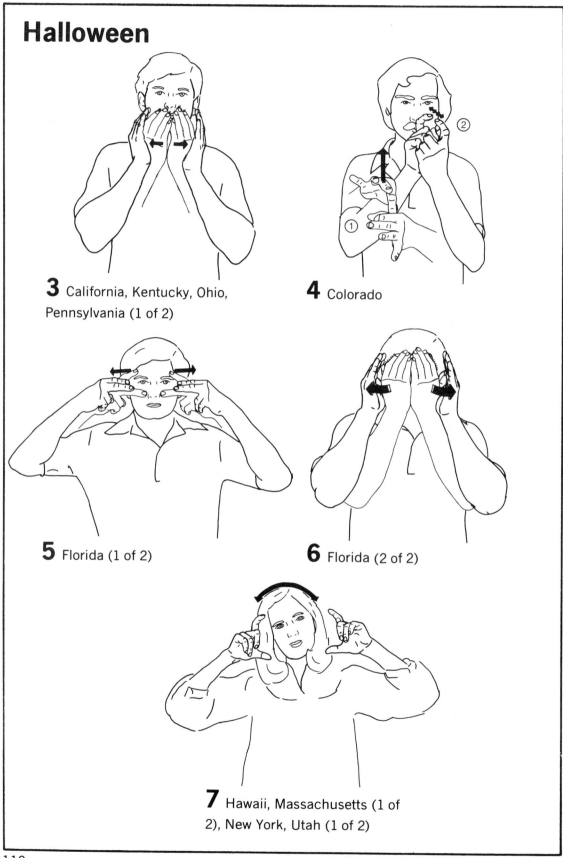

3 California, Kentucky, Ohio, Pennsylvania (1 of 2)

4 Colorado

5 Florida (1 of 2)

6 Florida (2 of 2)

7 Hawaii, Massachusetts (1 of 2), New York, Utah (1 of 2)

8 Illinois

+

9 Louisiana, North Carolina, Wisconsin

10 Maine

11 Massachusetts (2 of 2)

Halloween

12 Missouri, Utah (2 of 2)

13 North Dakota

14 Pennsylvania (2 of 2)

15 Texas

16 Virginia

17 Washington

hearing aid

Is your hearing aid new?

1 Alabama

2 Arkansas

3 California, Hawaii, North Carolina, Virginia

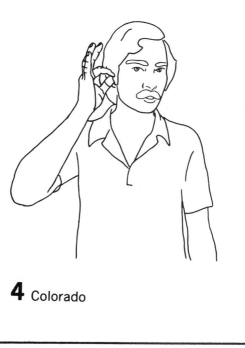

4 Colorado

113

hearing aid

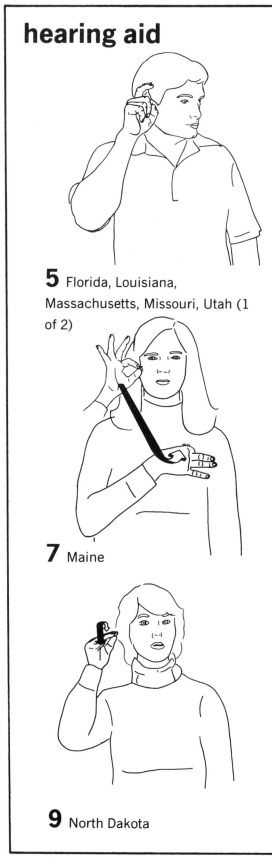

5 Florida, Louisiana, Massachusetts, Missouri, Utah (1 of 2)

6 Illinois, Kentucky, Michigan, New Mexico

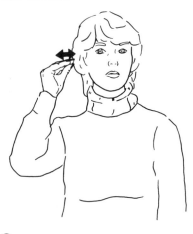
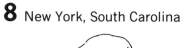

7 Maine

8 New York, South Carolina

9 North Dakota

10 Ohio

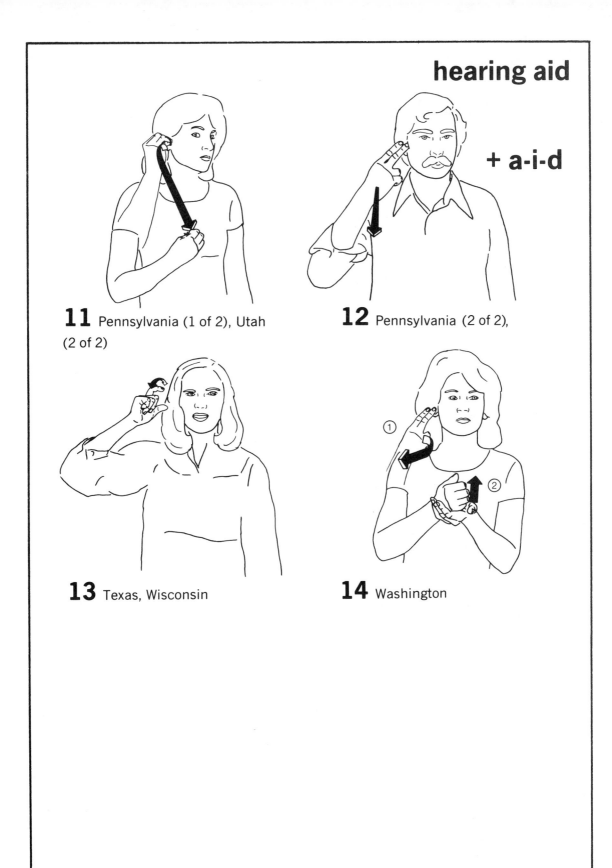

hearing aid

+ a-i-d

11 Pennsylvania (1 of 2), Utah (2 of 2)

12 Pennsylvania (2 of 2),

13 Texas, Wisconsin

14 Washington

heaven Do you believe in heaven and hell?

1 Alabama, Colorado

2 Arkansas, California, Illinois, Kentucky, Louisiana (1 of 2), Massachusetts, Missouri, New York (1 of 2), North Carolina, South Carolina, Texas

3 Florida, Hawaii (1 of 2), Maine, Michigan, New Mexico, North Dakota, Ohio, Pennsylvania (1 of 2), Utah, Virginia

4 Hawaii (2 of 2), Pennsylvania (2 of 2)

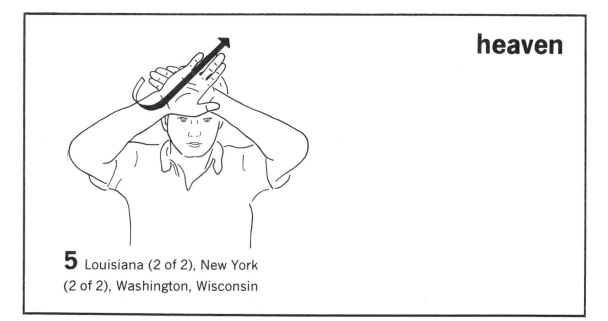

heaven

5 Louisiana (2 of 2), New York
(2 of 2), Washington, Wisconsin

hospital

The hospital emergency room is
always crowded.

1 Alabama (1 of 2), Arkansas,
California, Colorado, Florida,
Illinois, Kentucky,
Massachusetts, Michigan,
Missouri (1 of 2), New Mexico,
North Dakota, Ohio, Pennsylvania
(1 of 3), Texas, Utah,
Washington, Wisconsin

2 Alabama (2 of 2)

hospital

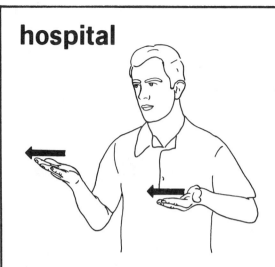 

3 Hawaii

4 Louisiana, North Carolina, South Carolina, Virginia

 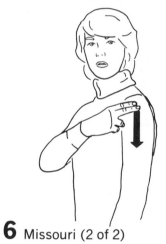

5 Maine

6 Missouri (2 of 2)

 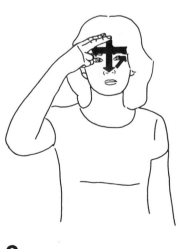

7 New York, Pennsylvania (2 of 3)

8 Pennsylvania (3 of 3)

hot dog

I had a hot dog with relish for lunch.

1 Alabama, Colorado, Louisiana, Maine, New Mexico, Ohio

2 Arkansas, Florida (1 of 2), Massachusetts, North Carolina

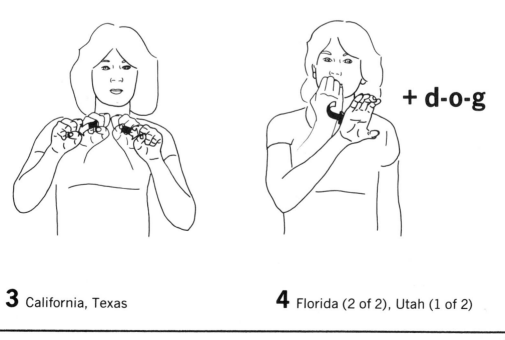

+ d-o-g

3 California, Texas

4 Florida (2 of 2), Utah (1 of 2)

hot dog

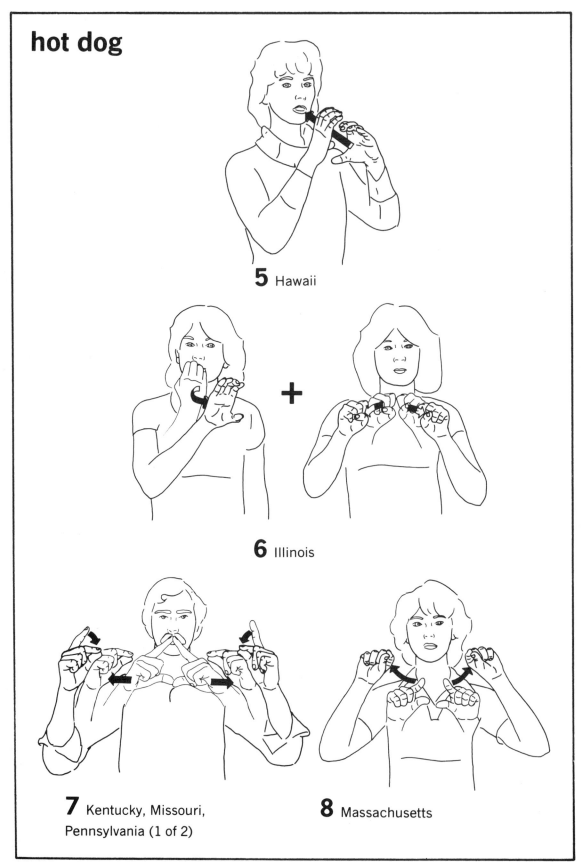

5 Hawaii

6 Illinois

7 Kentucky, Missouri, Pennsylvania (1 of 2)

8 Massachusetts

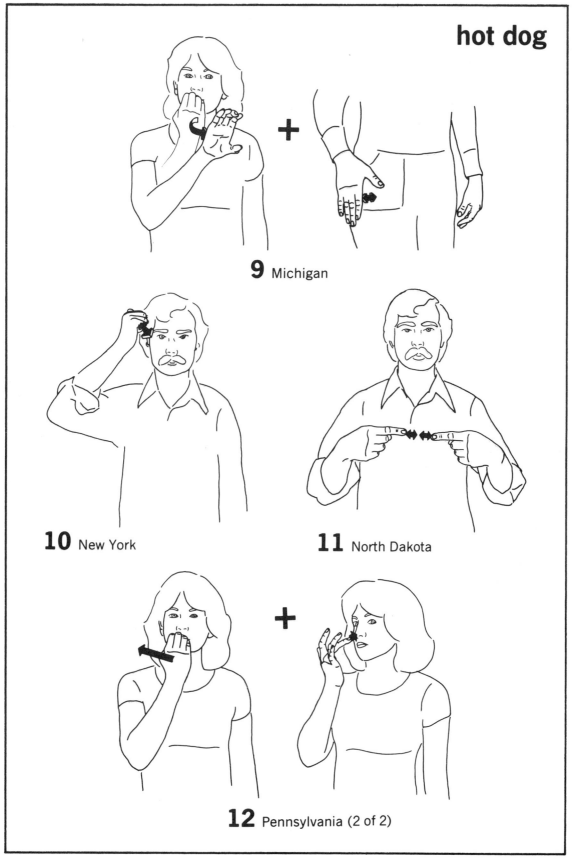

9 Michigan

10 New York

11 North Dakota

12 Pennsylvania (2 of 2)

hot dog

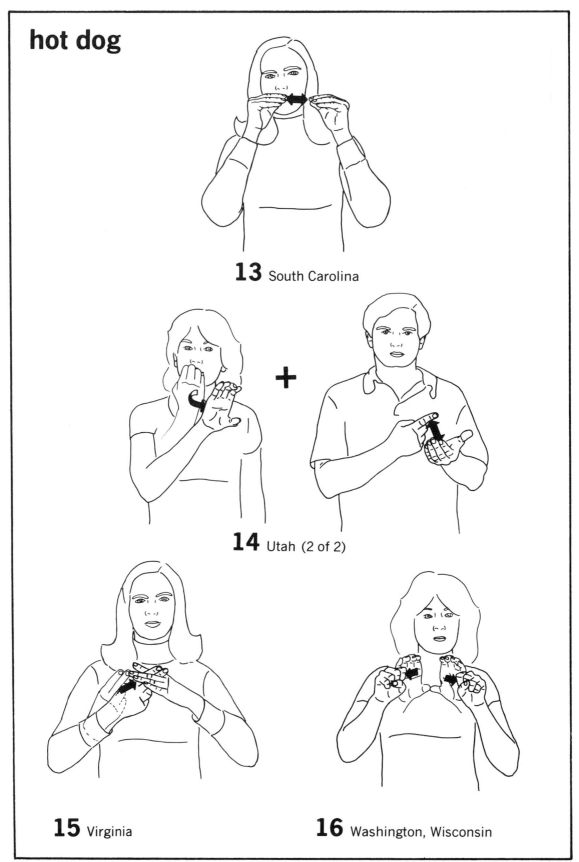

13 South Carolina

14 Utah (2 of 2)

15 Virginia

16 Washington, Wisconsin

hurt

My arm hurt after the tennis game.

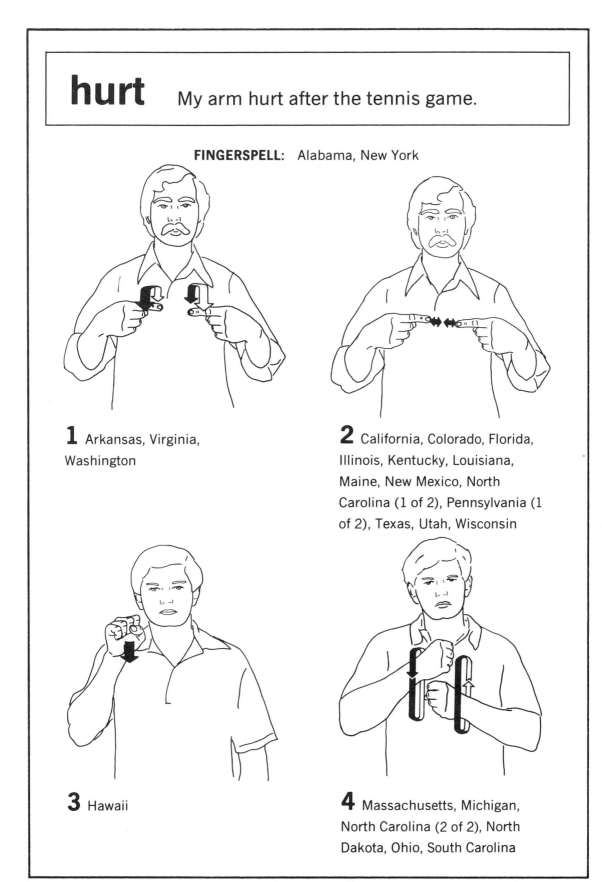

FINGERSPELL: Alabama, New York

1 Arkansas, Virginia, Washington

2 California, Colorado, Florida, Illinois, Kentucky, Louisiana, Maine, New Mexico, North Carolina (1 of 2), Pennsylvania (1 of 2), Texas, Utah, Wisconsin

3 Hawaii

4 Massachusetts, Michigan, North Carolina (2 of 2), North Dakota, Ohio, South Carolina

hurt

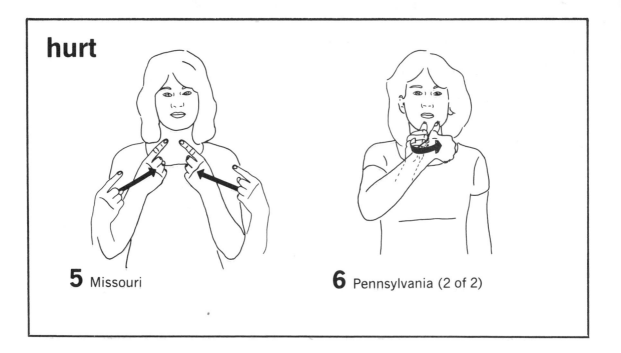

5 Missouri

6 Pennsylvania (2 of 2)

Indian

We visited an Indian reservation in Arizona.

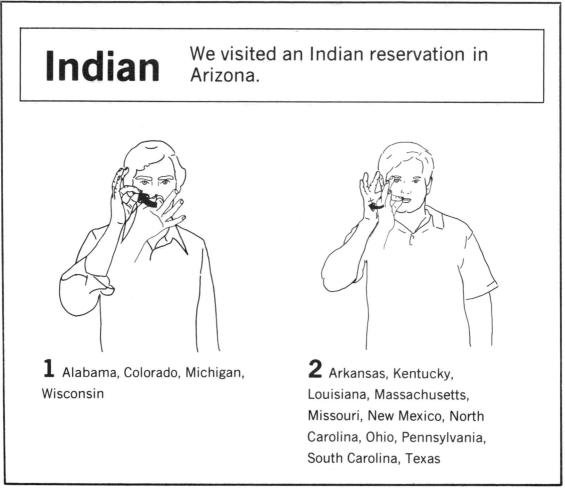

1 Alabama, Colorado, Michigan, Wisconsin

2 Arkansas, Kentucky, Louisiana, Massachusetts, Missouri, New Mexico, North Carolina, Ohio, Pennsylvania, South Carolina, Texas

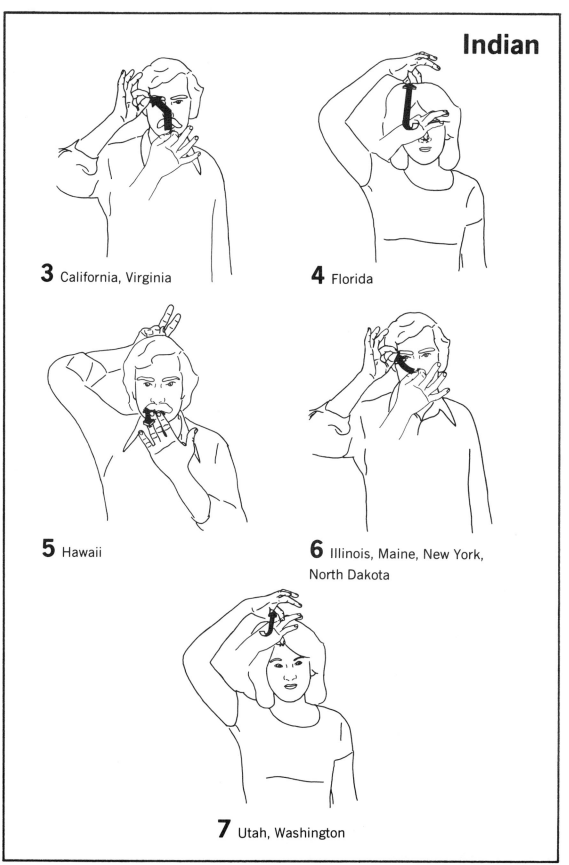

Indian

3 California, Virginia

4 Florida

5 Hawaii

6 Illinois, Maine, New York, North Dakota

7 Utah, Washington

interesting

He always tells interesting stories.

1 Alabama, Arkansas, Colorado, Illinois, Michigan, Missouri, Ohio

2 California, Kentucky, Louisiana, Massachusetts (1 of 2), New Mexico, New York, North Dakota, Pennsylvania (1 of 2), Texas, Utah (1 of 2), Virginia, Washington, Wisconsin

3 Florida, Massachusetts (2 of 2), Utah (2 of 2)

4 Hawaii

5 Maine

6 North Carolina, South Carolina

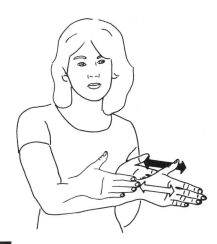

7 Pennsylvania (2 of 2)

Italian

I love Italian food.

FINGERSPELL: Hawaii, South Carolina

1 Alabama, Arkansas, California, Colorado, Illinois, Kentucky, Louisiana, Maine, Michigan, New Mexico, North Carolina, North Dakota, Ohio, Pennsylvania, Texas, Virginia, Wisconsin

2 Florida, Massachusetts (1 of 2), Missouri, Utah, Washington

3 Massachusetts (2 of 2)

4 New York

jam

She made 12 pints of cherry jam today.

FINGERSPELL: Alabama, California, New York, North Carolina, Ohio, South Carolina, Virginia, Wisconsin

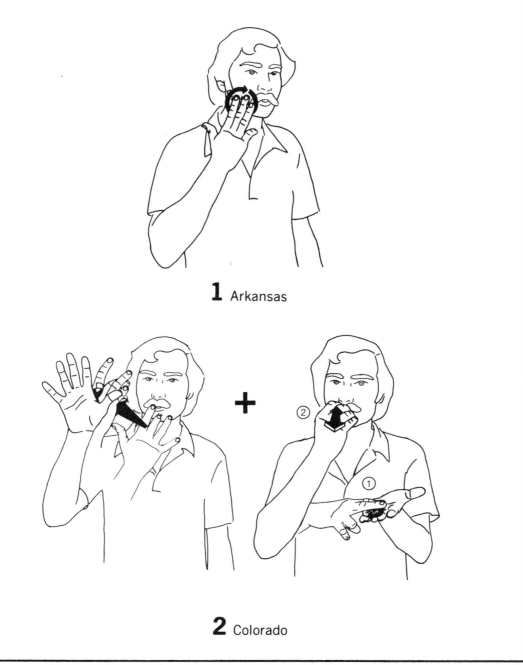

1 Arkansas

+

2 Colorado

jam

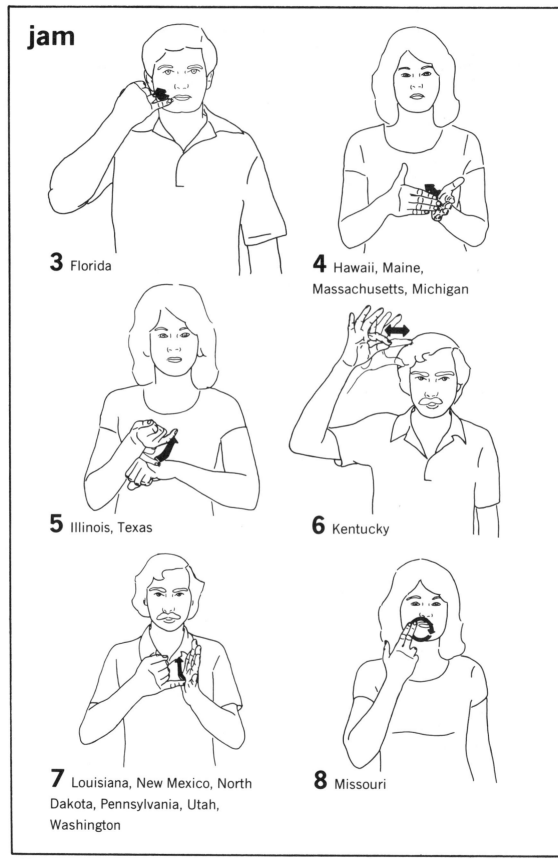

3 Florida

4 Hawaii, Maine, Massachusetts, Michigan

5 Illinois, Texas

6 Kentucky

7 Louisiana, New Mexico, North Dakota, Pennsylvania, Utah, Washington

8 Missouri

kid

That kid was in my class for three years.

FINGERSPELL: Maine

1 Alabama, Arkansas, Pennsylvania (1 of 2)

2 California, Florida, Illinois, Kentucky, Louisiana (1 of 2), Massachusetts, North Carolina, Utah, Wisconsin

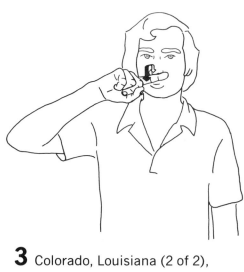

3 Colorado, Louisiana (2 of 2), New Mexico, North Dakota

4 Hawaii, Ohio, Pennsylvania (2 of 2), South Carolina

kid

5 Michigan, Missouri, New York, Texas, Washington

6 Virginia

kill   The fox killed some chickens.

FINGERSPELL: Wisconsin

1 Alabama

2 Arkansas, New Mexico

3 California, Illinois (1 of 2), North Carolina, North Dakota, Pennsylvania (1 of 3), Utah

4 Colorado, South Carolina

① ②

5 Florida, Illinois (2 of 2), Kentucky, Louisiana, Michigan, Missouri, New York, Pennsylvania (2 of 3), Texas, Virginia, Washington

6 Hawaii, Maine, Massachusetts

7 Ohio

8 Pennsylvania (3 of 3)

133

kitchen

They usually eat dinner in the kitchen.

FINGERSPELL: California

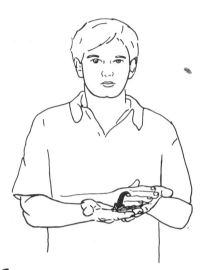

1 Alabama, Colorado, Massachusetts (1 of 2), Michigan, North Carolina, North Dakota, Ohio, South Carolina, Utah (1 of 2)

2 Arkansas, Florida, Illinois, Kentucky, Missouri, New Mexico, Texas, Utah (2 of 2), Virginia, Washington, Wisconsin

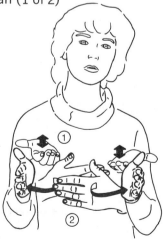

3 Hawaii

4 Louisiana, Massachusetts (2 of 2), Pennsylvania

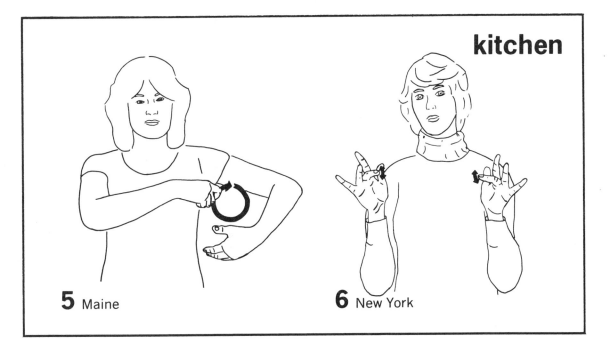

5 Maine

6 New York

lazy

Jim is too lazy to go jogging today.

1 Alabama, North Carolina, South Carolina, Virginia

2 Arkansas, California, Florida, Illinois, Kentucky, Maine, Missouri, New Mexico, North Dakota, Pennsylvania, Washington, Wisconsin

lazy

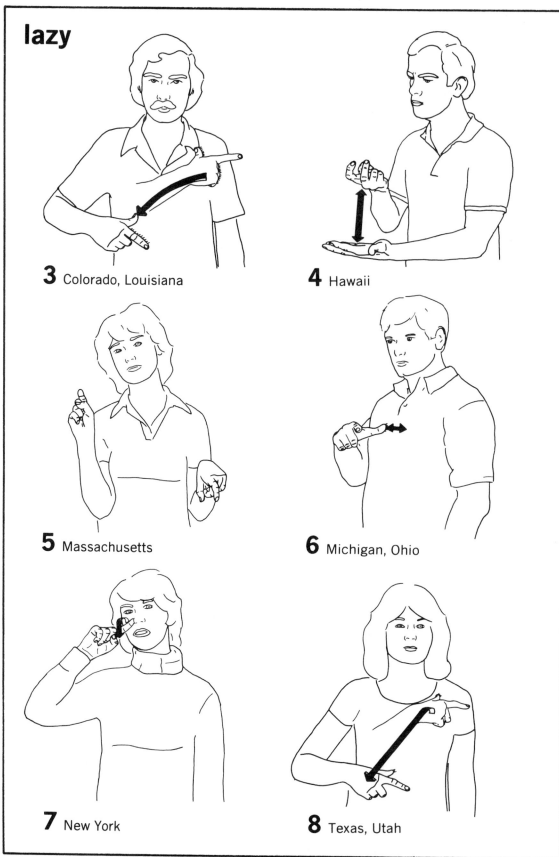

3 Colorado, Louisiana

4 Hawaii

5 Massachusetts

6 Michigan, Ohio

7 New York

8 Texas, Utah

light
The light by the front door is broken.

1 Alabama

2 Arkansas

3 California, Kentucky, Louisiana, New Mexico, New York, North Carolina, Utah

4 Colorado, Missouri, Wisconsin

light

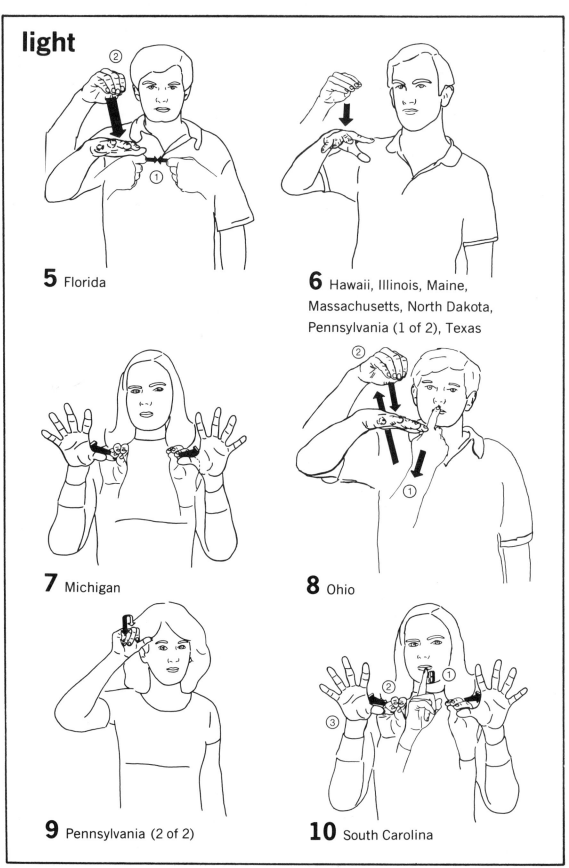

5 Florida

6 Hawaii, Illinois, Maine, Massachusetts, North Dakota, Pennsylvania (1 of 2), Texas

7 Michigan

8 Ohio

9 Pennsylvania (2 of 2)

10 South Carolina

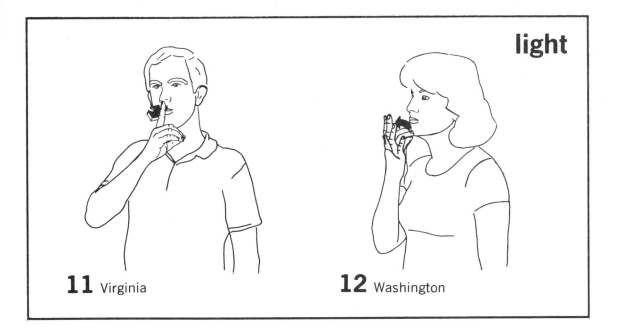

light

11 Virginia **12** Washington

lock

Someone broke the lock on the safe.

1 Alabama, Florida (1 of 2)

2 Arkansas

① ②

lock

3 California

+

4 Colorado, Illinois, Louisiana

5 Florida (2 of 2), Maine, Massachusetts, New Mexico, North Carolina, North Dakota, South Carolina, Texas, Utah, Virginia, Wisconsin

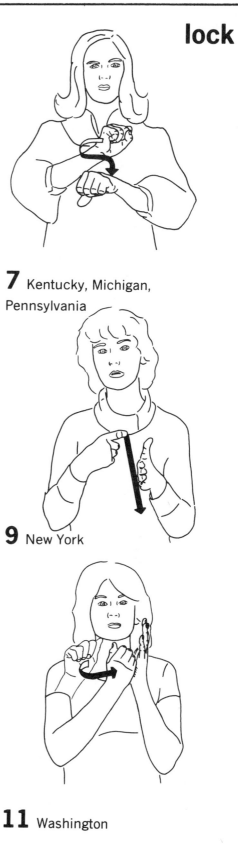

6 Hawaii

7 Kentucky, Michigan, Pennsylvania

8 Missouri

9 New York

10 Ohio

11 Washington

match
Your socks don't match.

FINGERSPELL: Illinois

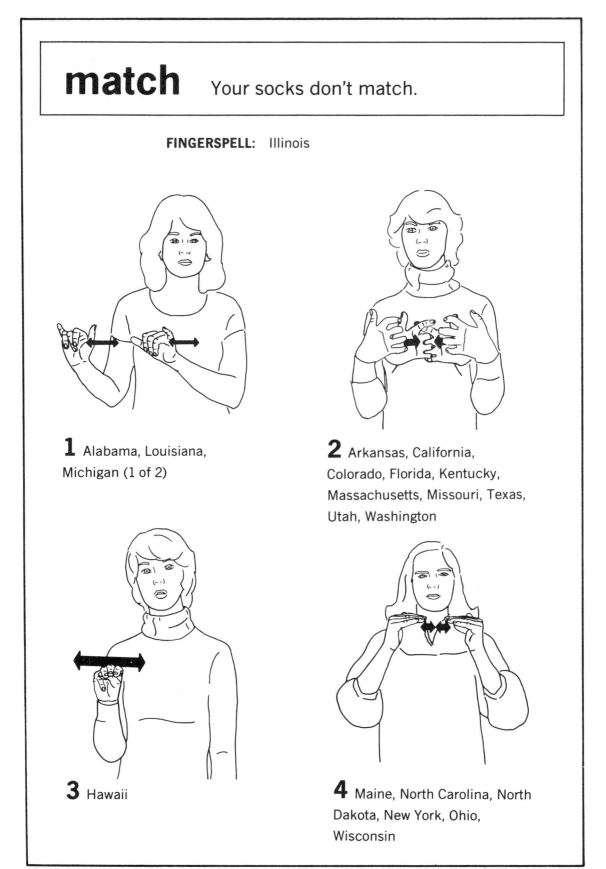

1 Alabama, Louisiana, Michigan (1 of 2)

2 Arkansas, California, Colorado, Florida, Kentucky, Massachusetts, Missouri, Texas, Utah, Washington

3 Hawaii

4 Maine, North Carolina, North Dakota, New York, Ohio, Wisconsin

5 Michigan (2 of 2)

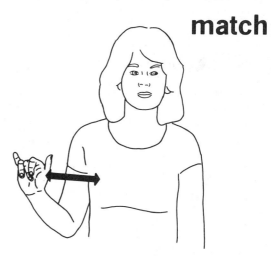

6 New Mexico, Pennsylvania (1 of 2), Virginia, South Carolina

7 Pennsylvania (2 of 2)

mean

Our neighbor is mean to the children.

1 Alabama, California, Missouri, Washington

2 Arkansas

3 Colorado, Michigan, North Carolina, Ohio, South Carolina, Texas, Virginia

4 Florida, Hawaii

mean

5 Illinois

6 Kentucky, Louisiana, New Mexico, North Dakota, Utah, Wisconsin

7 Maine

8 Massachusetts, Pennsylvania

9 New York

medicine

The medicine tasted awful, but it cured his cough.

1 Alabama

2 Arkansas, California, Colorado, Florida, Illinois, Kentucky, Louisiana, Maine, Massachusetts, Michigan, Missouri, New Mexico, New York, North Carolina, North Dakota, Pennsylvania (1 of 2), Texas, Utah, Washington, Wisconsin

3 Hawaii

4 Ohio, Pennsylvania (2 of 2)

5 South Carolina, Virginia

Monday

I work late on Monday afternoons.

1 Alabama, Arkansas, California, Colorado, Florida, Illinois, Kentucky, Louisiana, Maine, Massachusetts, Michigan, Missouri, New Mexico, New York, North Carolina (1 of 2), North Dakota, Ohio, Pennsylvania (1 of 2), South Carolina, Texas, Utah, Virginia, Washington, Wisconsin

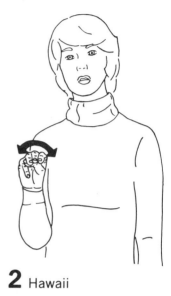

2 Hawaii

3 North Carolina (2 of 2), Pennsylvania (2 of 2)

movie

Our club rented a captioned movie.

1 Alabama, California, Colorado, Florida, Illinois, Kentucky, Louisiana (1 of 2), Maine, Massachusetts, Michigan, Missouri, New York, North Carolina, North Dakota, Pennsylvania (1 of 4), South Carolina, Texas, Utah, Virginia, Washington, Wisconsin (1 of 2)

2 Arkansas, Louisiana (2 of 2)

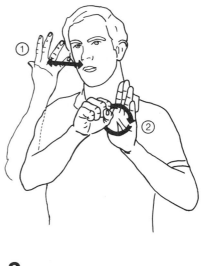

3 Hawaii, Ohio (1 of 2)

movie

4 New Mexico

5 Ohio (2 of 2)

6 Pennsylvania (2 of 4)

7 Pennsylvania (3 of 4)

8 Pennsylvania (4 of 4)

9 Wisconsin (2 of 2)

museum

We will visit the museum tomorrow.

FINGERSPELL: Alabama, California, Colorado, Florida, Hawaii, Illinois, Kentucky, Louisiana, Massachusetts, Michigan, Missouri, New Mexico, North Carolina, North Dakota, Ohio, South Carolina, Texas, Utah, Virginia, Washington, Wisconsin

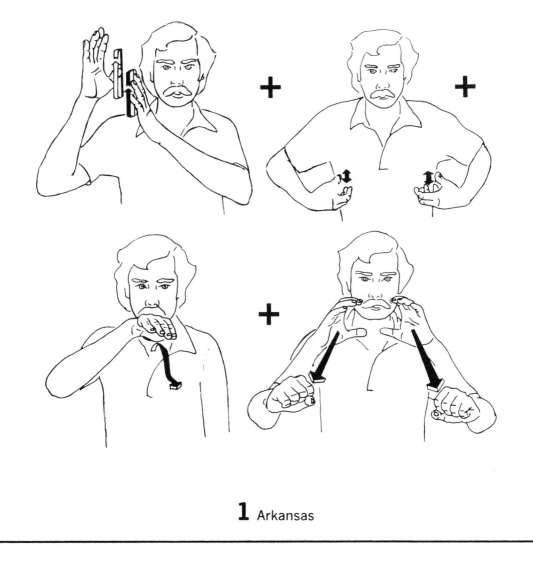

1 Arkansas

museum

2 Maine

3 New York

4 Pennsylvania

152

newspaper

He reads the newspaper
every morning on the train.

1 Alabama, Colorado, New York, Texas

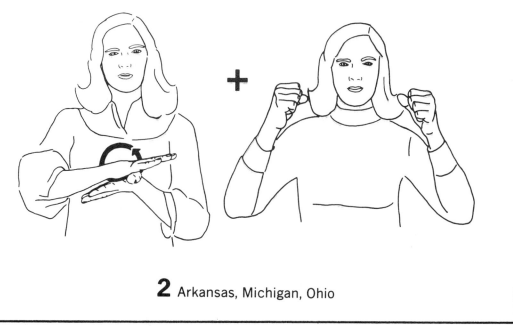

2 Arkansas, Michigan, Ohio

newspaper

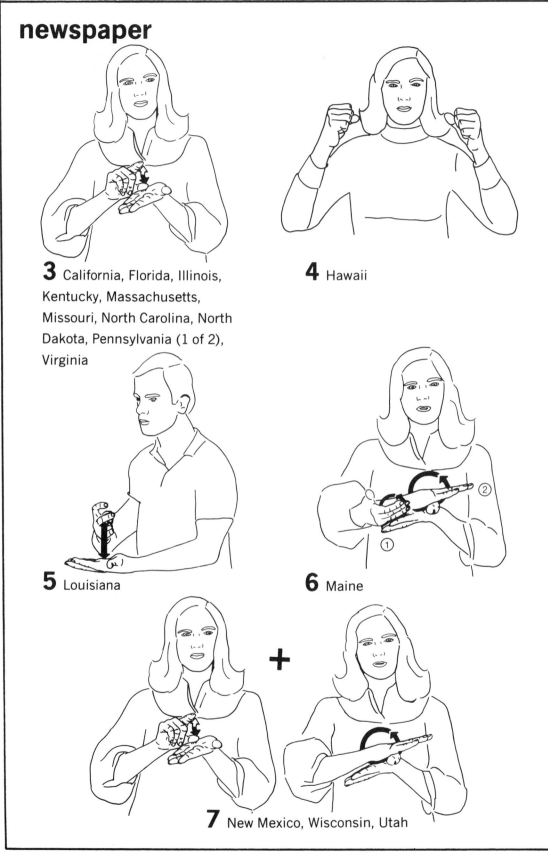

3 California, Florida, Illinois, Kentucky, Massachusetts, Missouri, North Carolina, North Dakota, Pennsylvania (1 of 2), Virginia

4 Hawaii

5 Louisiana

6 Maine

7 New Mexico, Wisconsin, Utah

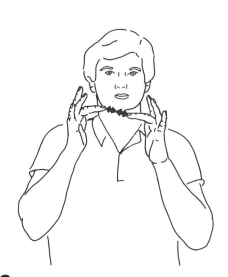

8 Pennsylvania (2 of 2)

n-e-w-s +

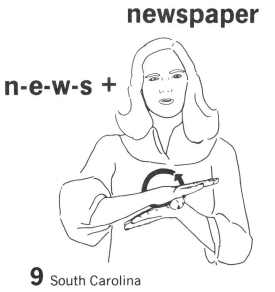

9 South Carolina

10 Washington

night

It is a dark night.

1 Alabama, Colorado, Illinois, Kentucky, Louisiana, Maine, Massachusetts, Michigan, New Mexico, North Carolina, North Dakota, Pennsylvania (1 of 2), Texas, Washington

2 Arkansas, California, Florida, Missouri, New York, Ohio, Utah, Wisconsin

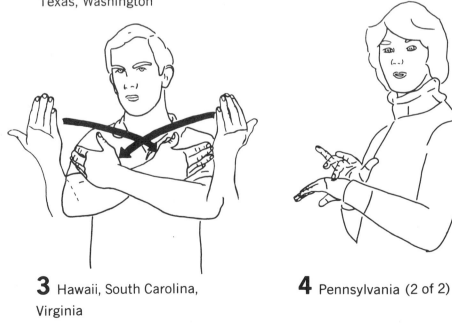

3 Hawaii, South Carolina, Virginia

4 Pennsylvania (2 of 2)

now   I must leave now.

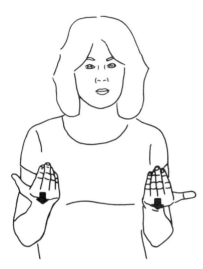

1 Alabama, Colorado, Illinois, Maine, Michigan, New Mexico, North Dakota, Ohio, Pennsylvania, Texas

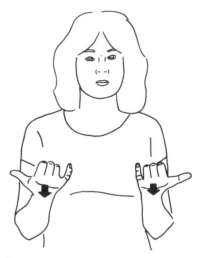

2 Arkansas, California, Florida, Kentucky, Louisiana, Massachusetts, Missouri, New York, North Carolina, South Carolina, Utah, Virginia, Washington, Wisconsin

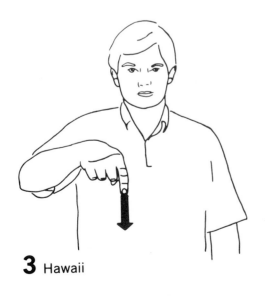

3 Hawaii

nurse The infirmary needs more nurses.

1 Alabama, Arkansas, California, Colorado, Florida, Illinois, Kentucky, Louisiana, Massachusetts, Michigan, Missouri, New Mexico, North Carolina, North Dakota, Pennsylvania (1 of 2), Texas, Utah, Washington, Wisconsin

2 Hawaii

3 Maine, New York, Ohio, Pennsylvania (2 of 2), South Carolina, Virginia

nuts   He eats a lot of nuts.

1 Alabama, California, Colorado, Florida, Illinois, Kentucky, Louisiana, Maine, Massachusetts, Missouri, New Mexico, New York, North Carolina, Ohio, Pennsylvania, South Carolina, Texas, Utah, Virginia, Washington

2 Arkansas, Wisconsin

3 Hawaii

4 Michigan

nuts

5 North Dakota

old   The old house needs to be painted.

1 Alabama, Arkansas, California, Colorado, Florida, Hawaii, Illinois, Kentucky, Louisiana, Maine, Massachusetts, Missouri, New Mexico, New York, North Carolina, North Dakota, Pennsylvania, South Carolina, Texas, Virginia, Washington, Wisconsin

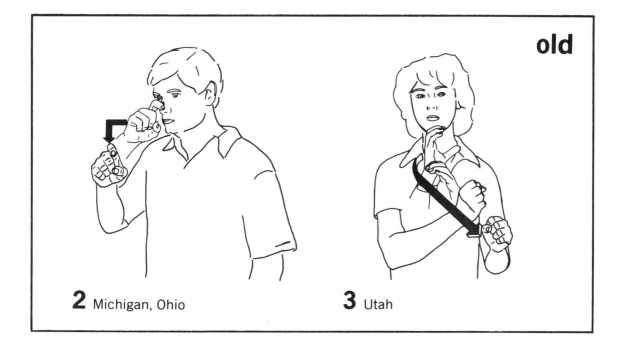

old

2 Michigan, Ohio

3 Utah

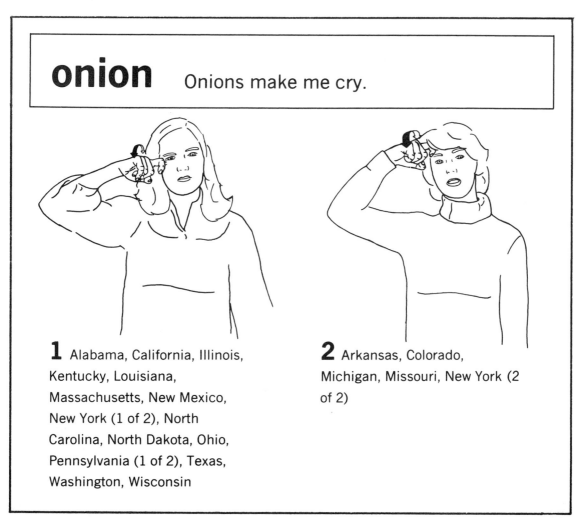

onion   Onions make me cry.

1 Alabama, California, Illinois, Kentucky, Louisiana, Massachusetts, New Mexico, New York (1 of 2), North Carolina, North Dakota, Ohio, Pennsylvania (1 of 2), Texas, Washington, Wisconsin

2 Arkansas, Colorado, Michigan, Missouri, New York (2 of 2)

onion

3 Florida, Pennsylvania (2 of 2), Utah

4 Hawaii

5 Maine

6 South Carolina, Virginia

orange

My favorite color is orange.

1 Alabama

2 Arkansas, North Dakota, Ohio, Pennsylvania (1 of 3)

3 California, Florida, Illinois, Louisiana, Maine, Massachusetts, Michigan, New York, North Carolina, Pennsylvania (2 of 3), Utah, Washington, Wisconsin

4 Colorado

orange

5 Hawaii

6 Kentucky

7 Missouri

8 New Mexico

9 Pennsylvania (3 of 3)

10 South Carolina, Virginia

orange

11 Texas

outside
The boys went outside to play.

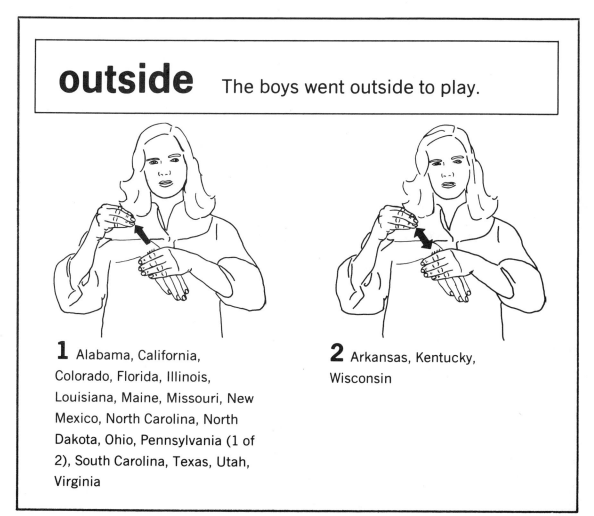

1 Alabama, California, Colorado, Florida, Illinois, Louisiana, Maine, Missouri, New Mexico, North Carolina, North Dakota, Ohio, Pennsylvania (1 of 2), South Carolina, Texas, Utah, Virginia

2 Arkansas, Kentucky, Wisconsin

outside

3 Hawaii

4 Massachusetts, Pennsylvania
(2 of 2)

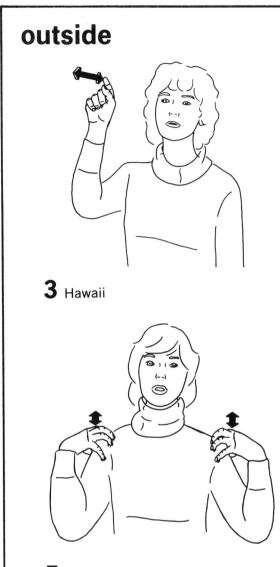

5 Michigan, New York

6 Washington

peach   I like peach pie.

FINGERSPELL: California, Maine, North Dakota

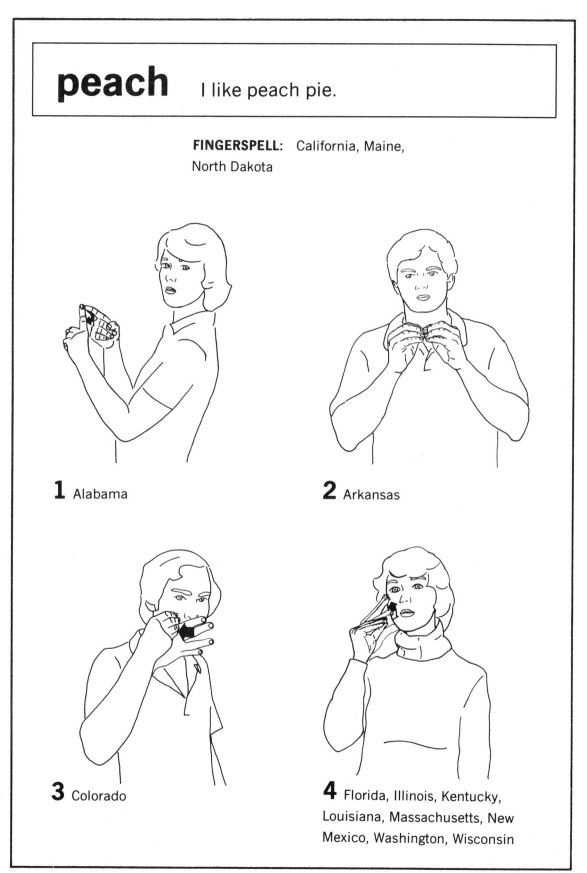

1 Alabama

2 Arkansas

3 Colorado

4 Florida, Illinois, Kentucky, Louisiana, Massachusetts, New Mexico, Washington, Wisconsin

peach

5 Hawaii

6 Michigan, South Carolina, Virginia

7 Missouri

8 New York

9 North Carolina, Utah

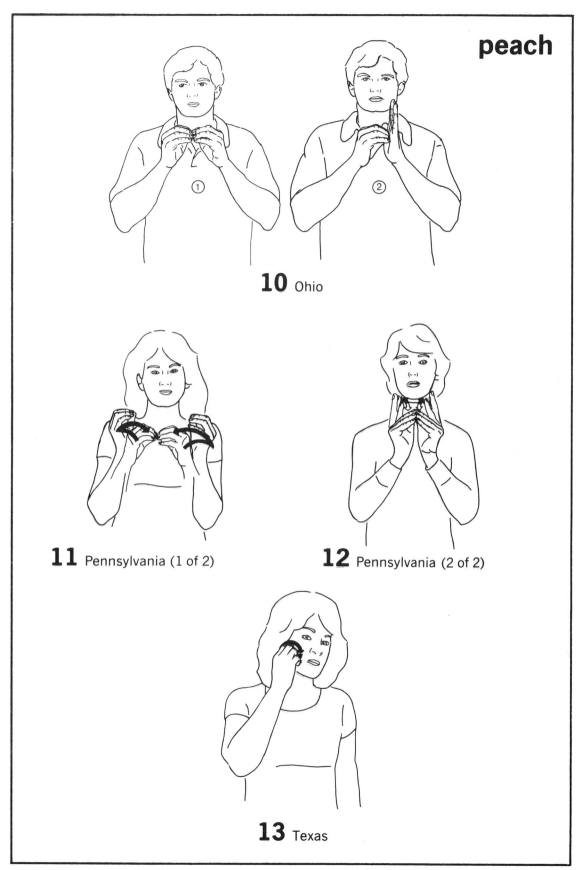

10 Ohio

11 Pennsylvania (1 of 2)

12 Pennsylvania (2 of 2)

13 Texas

peanut

Peanuts are a good source of protein.

1 Alabama, Maine, South Carolina, Virginia

2 Arkansas

3 California, Florida, Kentucky, Louisiana, Massachusetts, Michigan, Missouri, New York, North Carolina, Ohio, Utah, Wisconsin (1 of 2)

4 Colorado, Pennsylvania

peanut

5 Hawaii, Wisconsin (2 of 2)

6 Illinois, New Mexico

7 North Dakota

8 Texas

9 Washington

pear

The pear is the freshest fruit on the plate.

FINGERSPELL: Alabama, California, North Dakota, Pennsylvania, South Carolina, Texas, Virginia

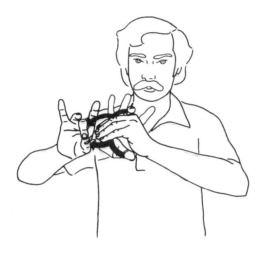

1 Arkansas

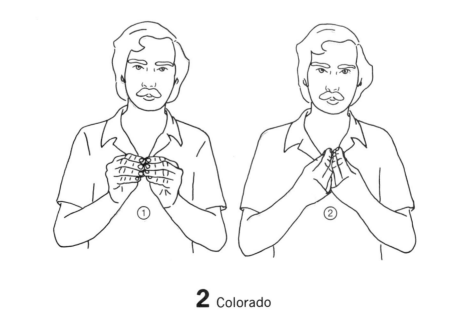

2 Colorado

3 Florida, Illinois, Kentucky,
Louisiana, North Carolina,
Washington, Wisconsin

4 Hawaii

5 Maine

6 Massachusetts

7 Michigan

8 Missouri, New York

173

pear

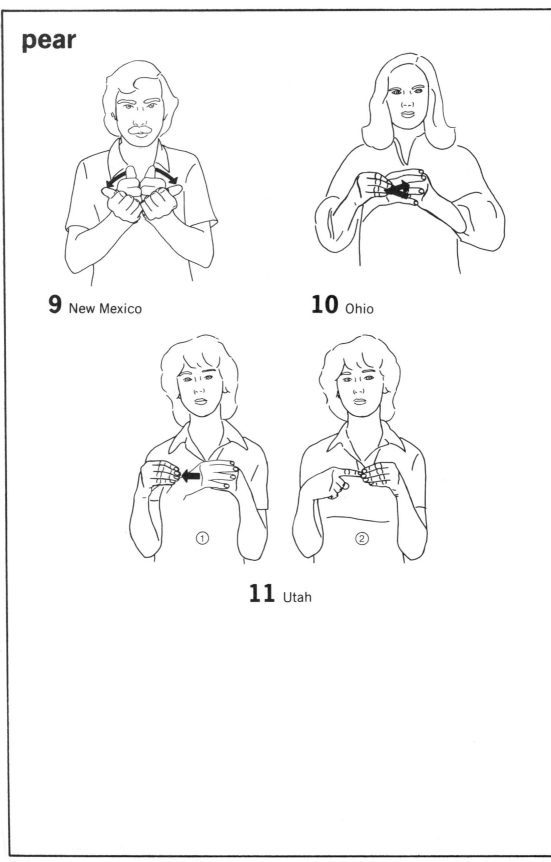

9 New Mexico

10 Ohio

11 Utah

①

②

174

perfume

French perfume is expensive.

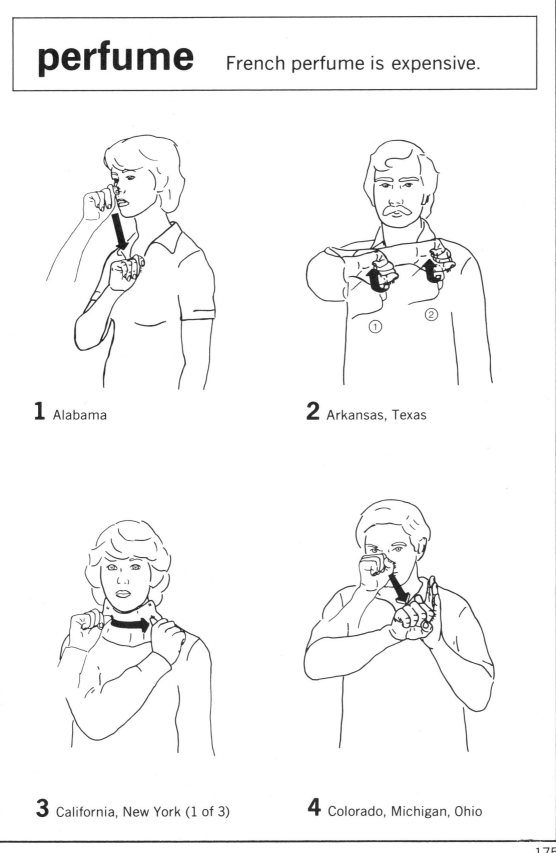

1 Alabama

2 Arkansas, Texas

3 California, New York (1 of 3)

4 Colorado, Michigan, Ohio

perfume

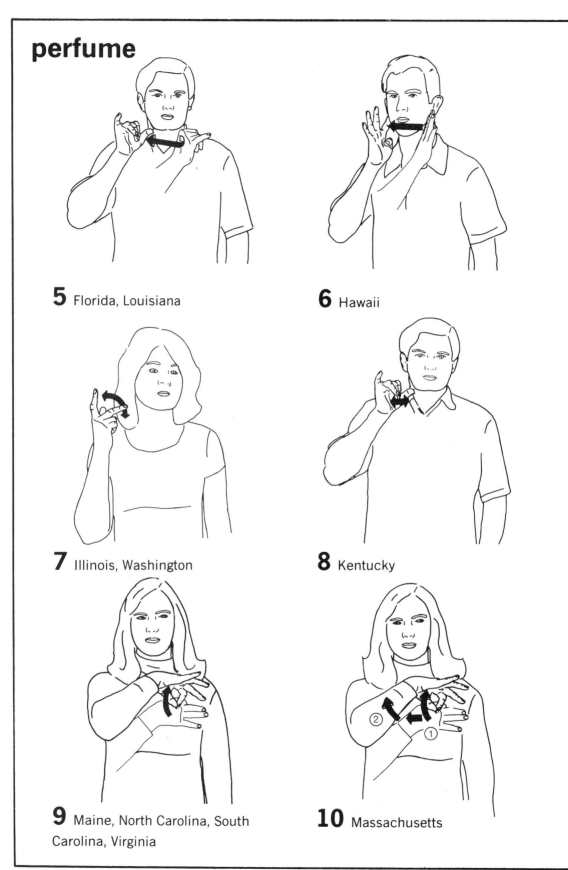

5 Florida, Louisiana

6 Hawaii

7 Illinois, Washington

8 Kentucky

9 Maine, North Carolina, South Carolina, Virginia

10 Massachusetts

11 Missouri

12 New Mexico

13 New York (2 of 3)

14 New York (3 of 3)

15 North Dakota, Pennsylvania

16 Utah

perfume

17 Wisconsin

picnic

The picnic was canceled because of the storm.

FINGERSPELL: Louisiana, Maine, Virginia

1 Alabama

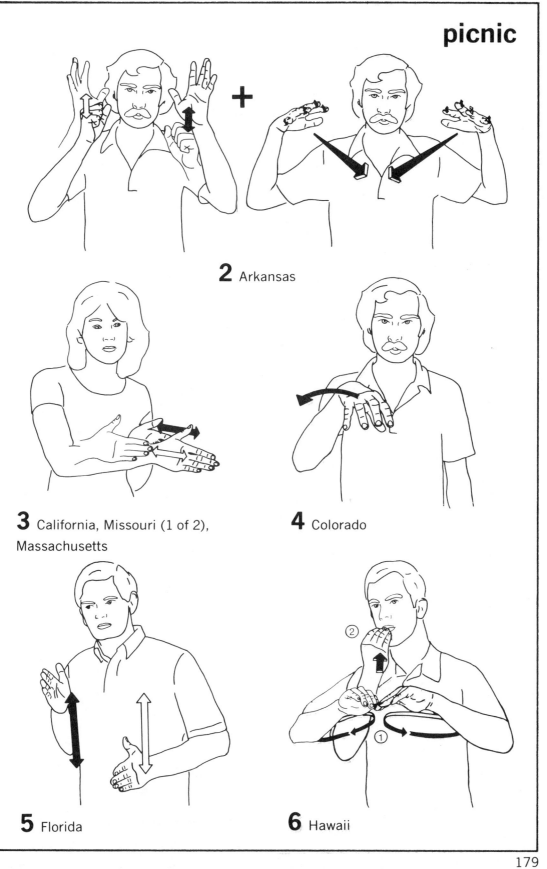

picnic

2 Arkansas

3 California, Missouri (1 of 2), Massachusetts

4 Colorado

5 Florida

6 Hawaii

picnic

7 Illinois (1 of 2)

8 Illinois (2 of 2), Missouri (2 of 2)

9 Kentucky

10 Michigan

11 New Mexico

12 New York (1 of 2)

180

13 New York (2 of 2)

14 North Carolina

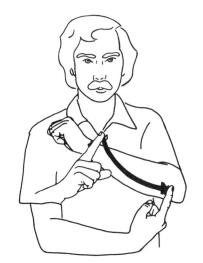

15 North Dakota

16 Ohio

17 Pennsylvania

18 South Carolina

picnic

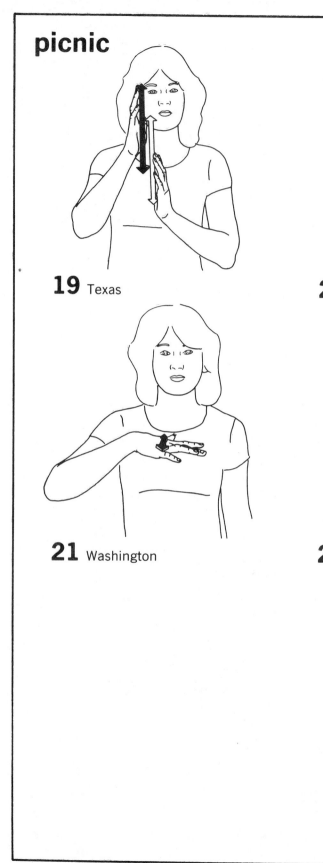

19 Texas

20 Utah

21 Washington

22 Wisconsin

picture

The picture of the parade won a prize.

FINGERSPELL: Maine

1 Alabama, Arkansas, California, Colorado, Florida, Illinois, Kentucky, Louisiana, Massachusetts, Michigan, New Mexico, New York, North Carolina, North Dakota, Pennsylvania (1 of 2), South Carolina, Texas, Utah, Virginia, Washington, Wisconsin

2 Hawaii

3 Missouri

4 Ohio, Pennsylvania (2 of 2)

pink

She bought a pink dress.

1 Alabama

2 Arkansas, California, Colorado, Florida, Illinois, Kentucky, Missouri, New Mexico, North Carolina, North Dakota, South Carolina, Texas, Utah, Virginia, Wisconsin

3 Hawaii

4 Louisiana, New York

5 Maine, Washington

6 Massachusetts, Pennsylvania (1 of 2)

7 Michigan, Ohio

8 Pennsylvania (2 of 2)

pizza

Order a pizza for me.

FINGERSPELL: Alabama, California, Colorado, Florida, Illinois, Kentucky, Maine, Michigan, Missouri, North Carolina, North Dakota, Ohio, South Carolina, Texas, Virginia, Wisconsin

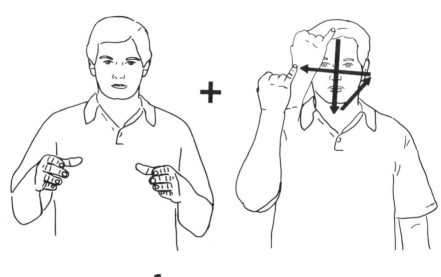

1 Arkansas, Utah

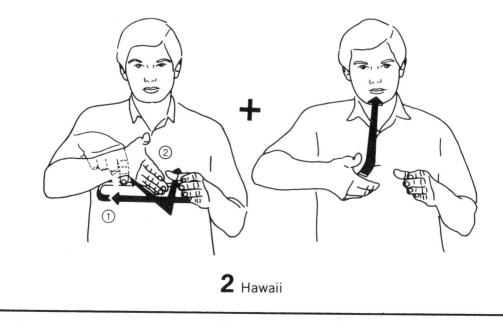

2 Hawaii

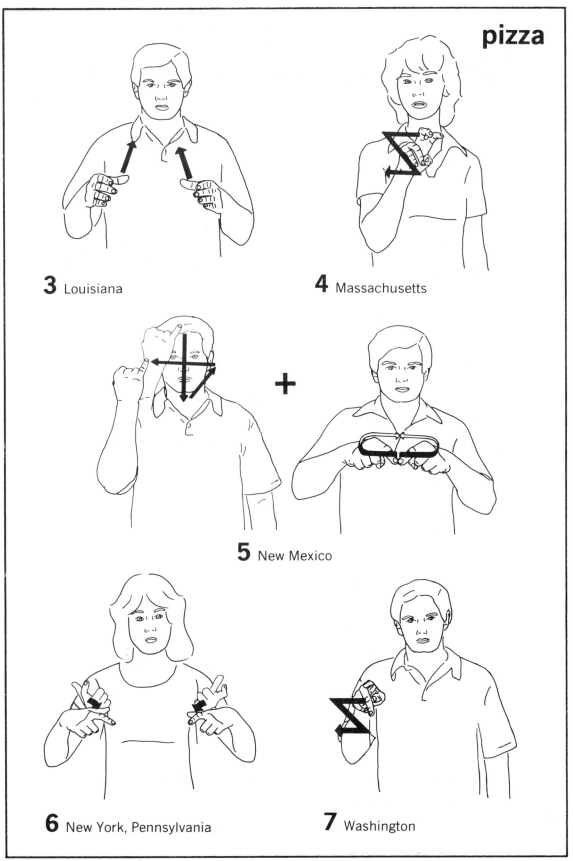

pizza

3 Louisiana

4 Massachusetts

5 New Mexico

6 New York, Pennsylvania

7 Washington

police

The police found the missing child.

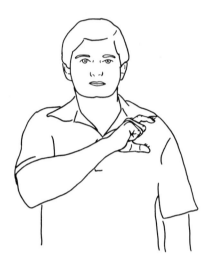

1 Alabama, Arkansas, California, Colorado, Hawaii, Kentucky, Maine, Massachusetts, New Mexico, New York, North Carolina, Pennsylvania (1 of 2), Utah, Virginia, Washington

2 Florida, Louisiana, Missouri (1 of 2), North Dakota, Pennsylvania (2 of 2), Texas

3 Illinois (1 of 2), Michigan, Missouri (2 of 2), Ohio, South Carolina, Wisconsin

4 Illinois (2 of 2)

pop Some people say soda instead of pop.

FINGERSPELL: Alabama, Florida, Maine

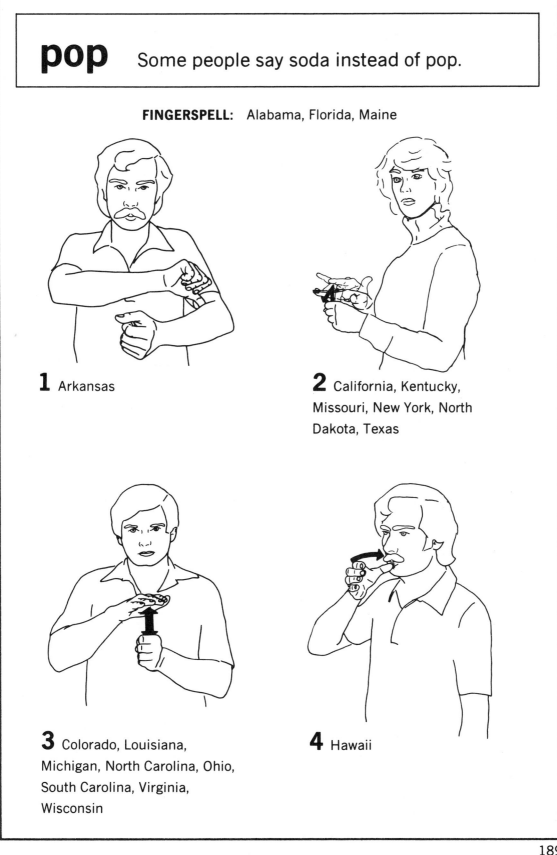

1 Arkansas

2 California, Kentucky, Missouri, New York, North Dakota, Texas

3 Colorado, Louisiana, Michigan, North Carolina, Ohio, South Carolina, Virginia, Wisconsin

4 Hawaii

pop

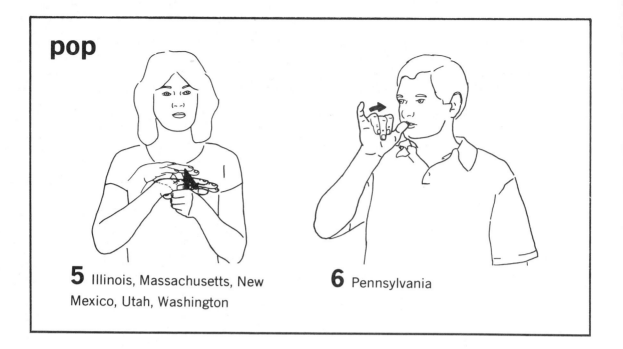

5 Illinois, Massachusetts, New Mexico, Utah, Washington

6 Pennsylvania

pregnant
My wife is pregnant.

FINGERSPELL p-g or p-r-e-g: Illinois (1 of 2)

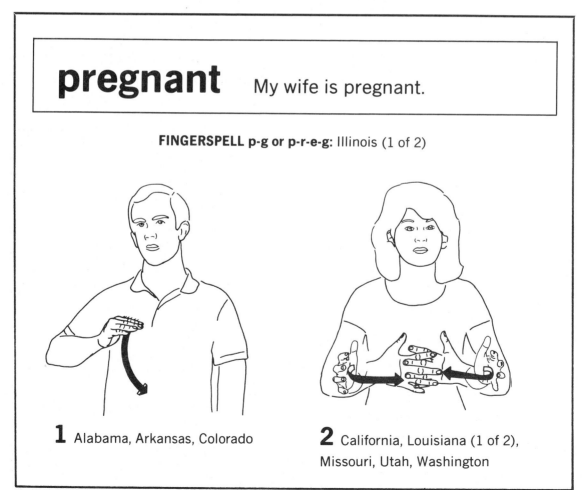

1 Alabama, Arkansas, Colorado

2 California, Louisiana (1 of 2), Missouri, Utah, Washington

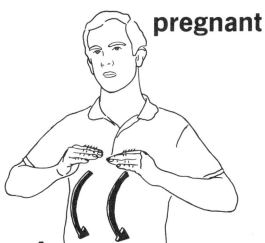

3 Florida, Kentucky, Ohio, Pennsylvania (1 of 3)

4 Hawaii, Illinois (2 of 2), North Dakota

5 Louisiana (2 of 2), New Mexico, New York, Texas

6 Maine, Massachusetts

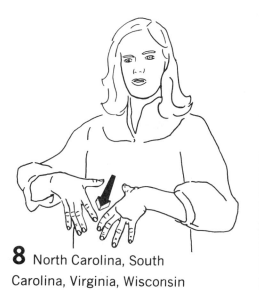

7 Michigan

8 North Carolina, South Carolina, Virginia, Wisconsin

191

pregnant

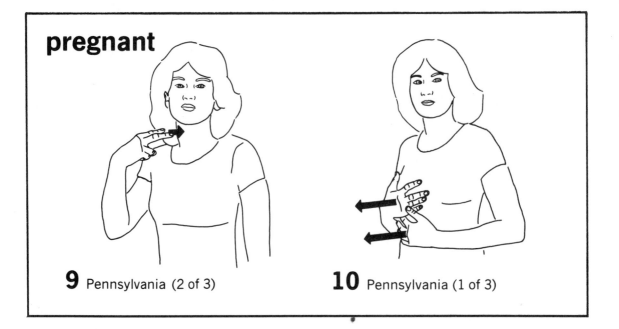

9 Pennsylvania (2 of 3)

10 Pennsylvania (1 of 3)

purple

They found wallpaper to match the purple curtains.

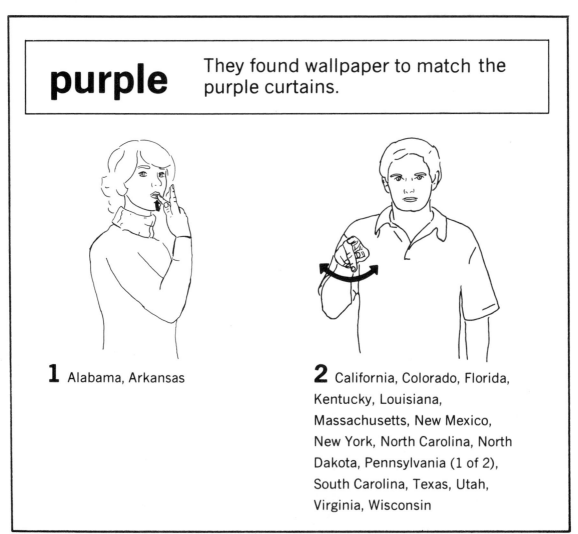

1 Alabama, Arkansas

2 California, Colorado, Florida, Kentucky, Louisiana, Massachusetts, New Mexico, New York, North Carolina, North Dakota, Pennsylvania (1 of 2), South Carolina, Texas, Utah, Virginia, Wisconsin

3 Hawaii

4 Illinois, Washington

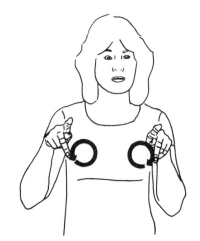

5 Maine

6 Michigan, Missouri, Ohio

7 Pennsylvania (2 of 2)

rabbit

The rabbit ate the lettuce in my garden.

FINGERSPELL: Maine

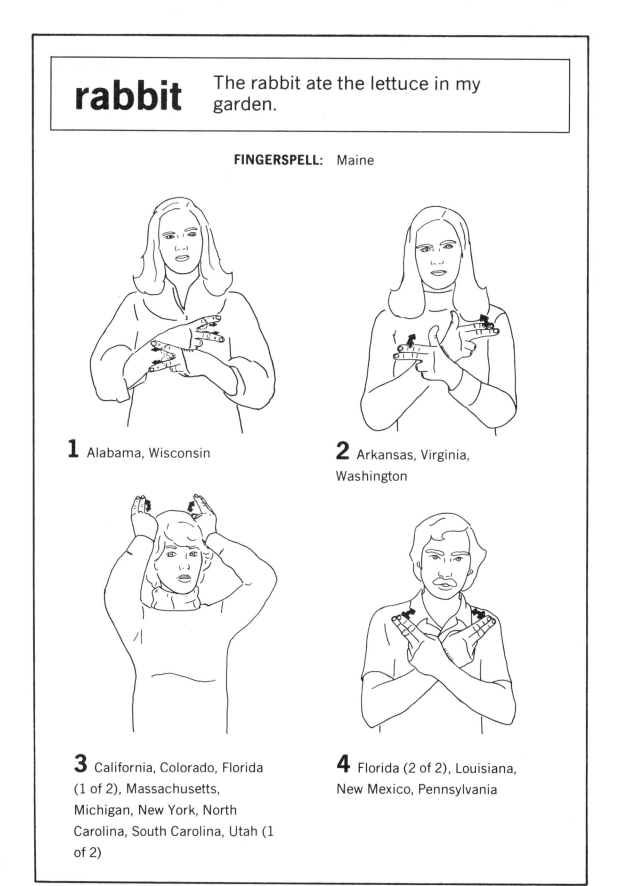

1 Alabama, Wisconsin

2 Arkansas, Virginia, Washington

3 California, Colorado, Florida (1 of 2), Massachusetts, Michigan, New York, North Carolina, South Carolina, Utah (1 of 2)

4 Florida (2 of 2), Louisiana, New Mexico, Pennsylvania

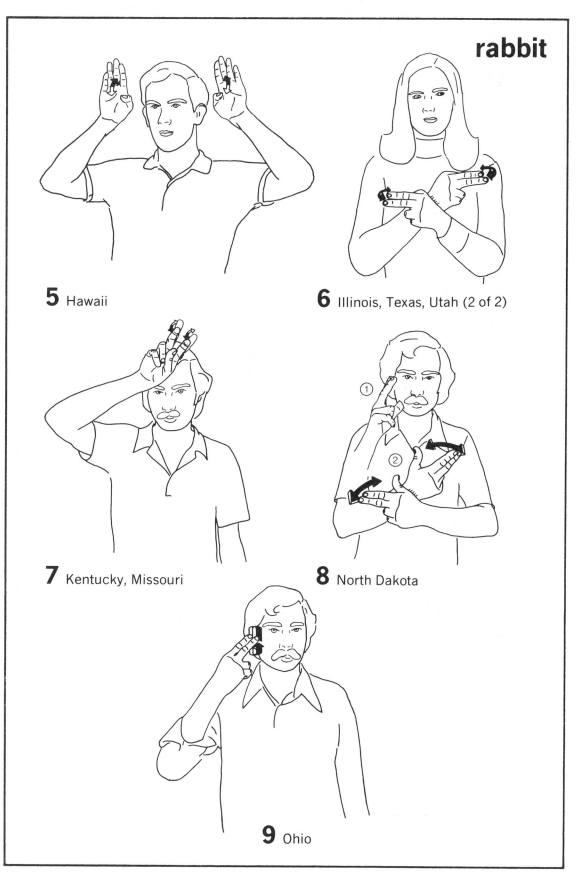

5 Hawaii

6 Illinois, Texas, Utah (2 of 2)

7 Kentucky, Missouri

8 North Dakota

9 Ohio

rather

What would you rather do—go bowling or go to the movies?

FINGERSPELL: Colorado, Maine, Michigan, South Carolina, Texas, Virginia, Washington

1 Alabama, Florida

2 Arkansas, New Mexico

3 California, Illinois (1 of 2), Louisiana (1 of 2), Massachusetts, Missouri, North Carolina

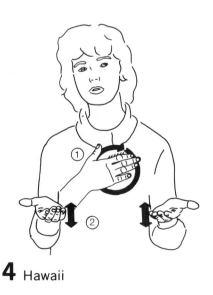

4 Hawaii

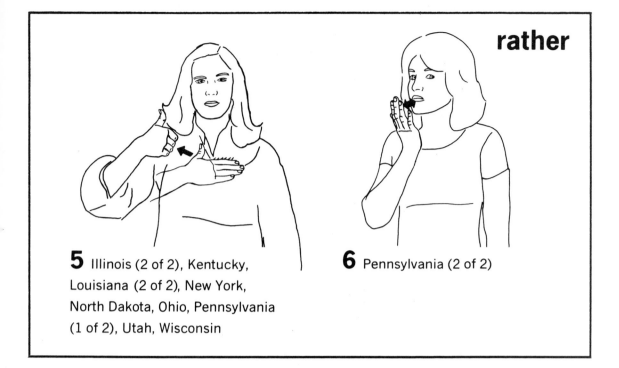

rather

5 Illinois (2 of 2), Kentucky, Louisiana (2 of 2), New York, North Dakota, Ohio, Pennsylvania (1 of 2), Utah, Wisconsin

6 Pennsylvania (2 of 2)

rest   Rest here for ten minutes.

1 Alabama, Arkansas, California, Hawaii, Illinois, Louisiana, Maine, North Dakota, Utah, Virginia, Wisconsin

2 Colorado, Michigan, New Mexico, North Carolina, Ohio, South Carolina

rest

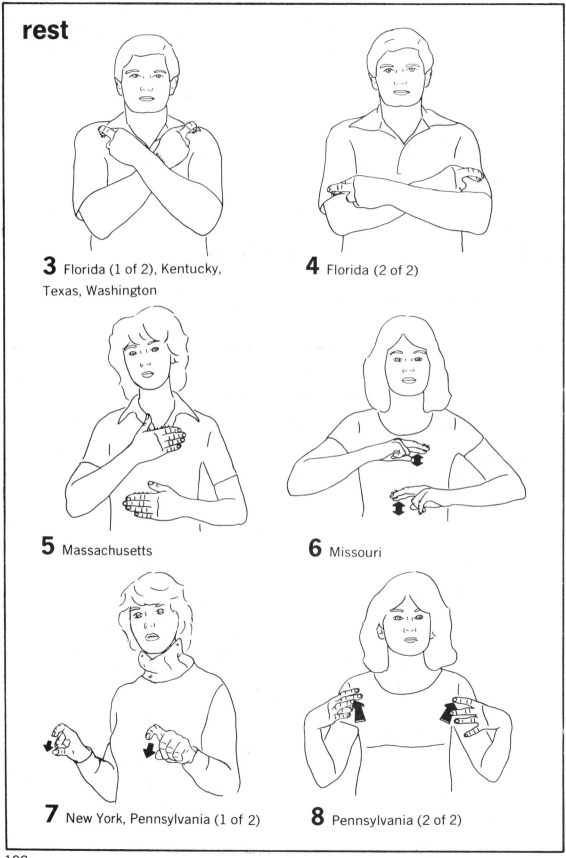

3 Florida (1 of 2), Kentucky, Texas, Washington

4 Florida (2 of 2)

5 Massachusetts

6 Missouri

7 New York, Pennsylvania (1 of 2)

8 Pennsylvania (2 of 2)

run
He runs a mile every day.

1 Alabama, Arkansas, Florida, Illinois, Kentucky, Louisiana (1 of 2), Massachusetts, New Mexico, New York, Ohio, Virginia

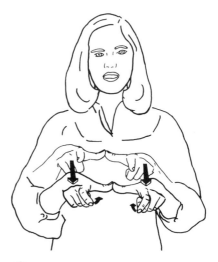

2 California, Colorado, Missouri, North Dakota, Pennsylvania, Utah, Washington, Wisconsin

3 Hawaii, Louisiana (2 of 2)

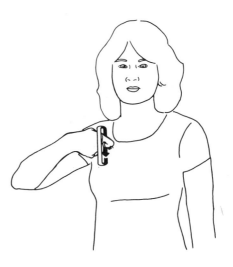

4 Maine

run

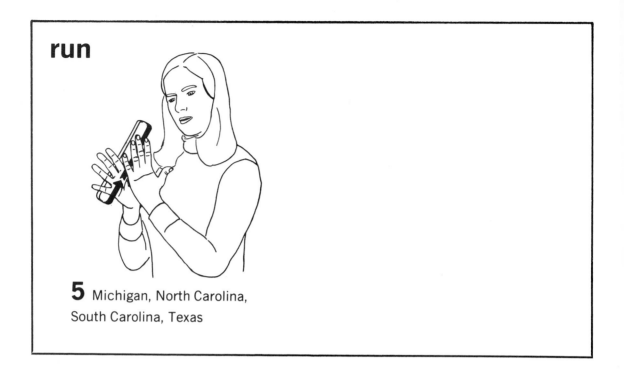

5 Michigan, North Carolina, South Carolina, Texas

sandwich He ate three bologna sandwiches for lunch.

1 Alabama, Arkansas, Colorado, Kentucky, New Mexico, North Carolina, North Dakota, South Carolina, Texas, Virginia, Washington

2 California, Florida, New York

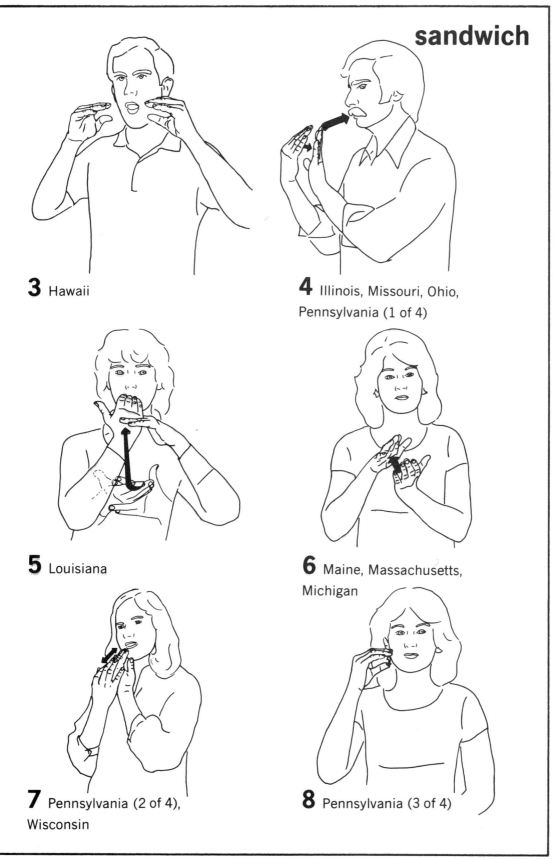

sandwich

3 Hawaii

4 Illinois, Missouri, Ohio,
Pennsylvania (1 of 4)

5 Louisiana

6 Maine, Massachusetts,
Michigan

7 Pennsylvania (2 of 4),
Wisconsin

8 Pennsylvania (3 of 4)

sandwich

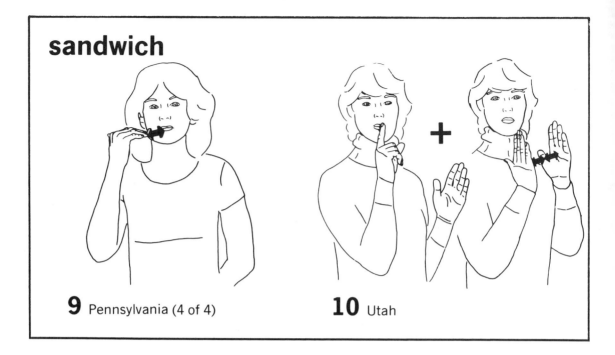

9 Pennsylvania (4 of 4)   **10** Utah

Santa Claus

She wrote a letter to Santa Claus.

1 Alabama, Texas   **2** Arkansas

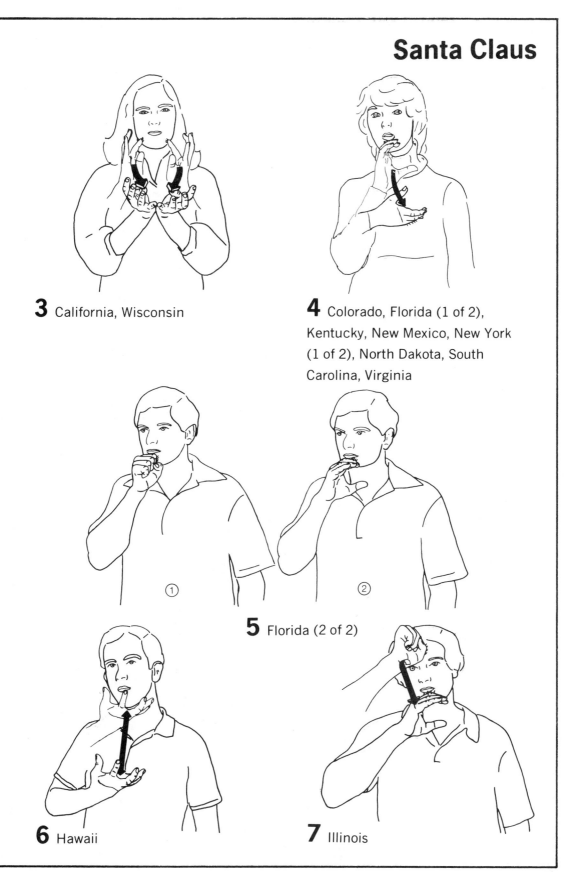

Santa Claus

3 California, Wisconsin

4 Colorado, Florida (1 of 2), Kentucky, New Mexico, New York (1 of 2), North Dakota, South Carolina, Virginia

①

②

5 Florida (2 of 2)

6 Hawaii

7 Illinois

Santa Claus

8 Louisiana

9 Maine

10 Massachusetts, Utah, Washington

11 Michigan

12 Missouri

13 New York (2 of 2)

Santa Claus

14 North Carolina (1 of 2), Ohio, Pennsylvania

15 North Carolina (2 of 2)

Saturday

Saturday is my day off.

1 Alabama, Arkansas, California, Colorado, Florida, Illinois, Kentucky, Louisiana, Maine, Massachusetts, Michigan, Missouri, New Mexico, New York North Carolina (1 of 2), North

2 Hawaii

Dakota, Ohio, Pennsylvania (1 of 2), South Carolina, Texas, Utah, Virginia, Washington, Wisconsin

Saturday

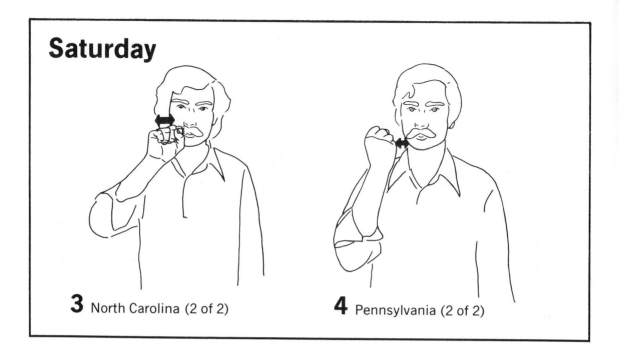

3 North Carolina (2 of 2)

4 Pennsylvania (2 of 2)

shoes   My shoes are too tight.

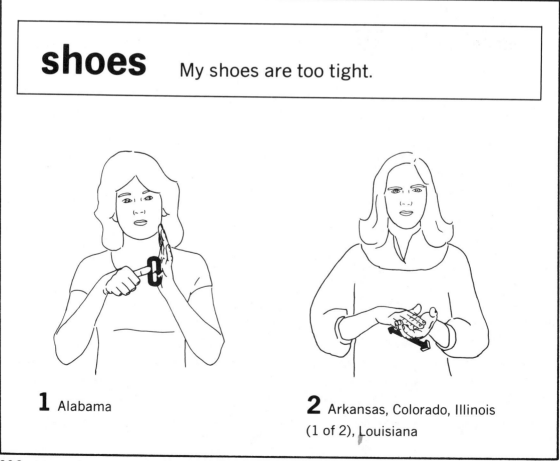

1 Alabama

2 Arkansas, Colorado, Illinois (1 of 2), Louisiana

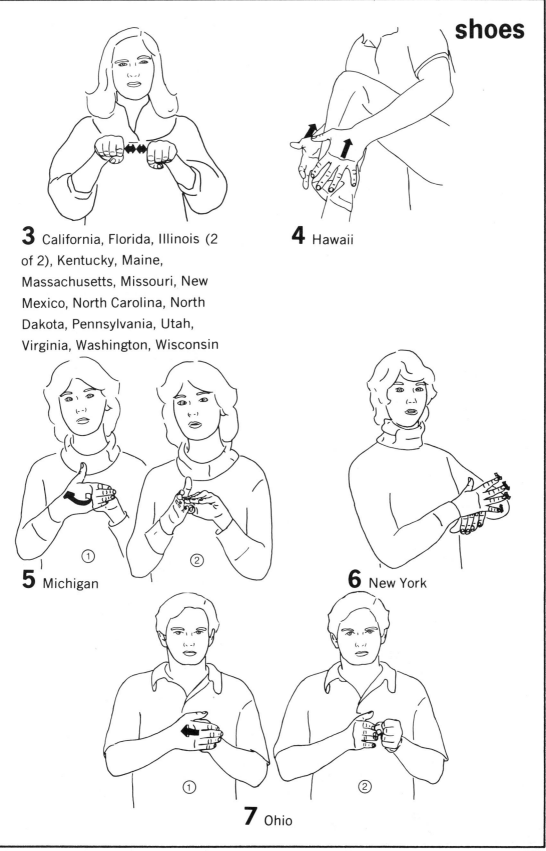

shoes

3 California, Florida, Illinois (2 of 2), Kentucky, Maine, Massachusetts, Missouri, New Mexico, North Carolina, North Dakota, Pennsylvania, Utah, Virginia, Washington, Wisconsin

4 Hawaii

5 Michigan

6 New York

7 Ohio

shoes

8 South Carolina, Texas

slippers His slippers match his bathrobe.

FINGERSPELL: Arkansas, California, North Carolina

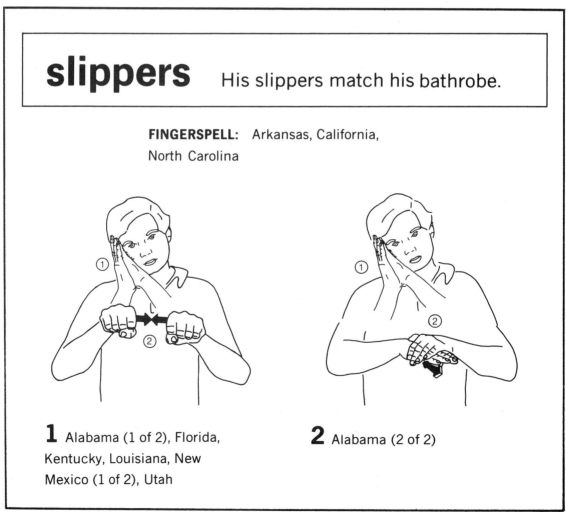

1 Alabama (1 of 2), Florida, Kentucky, Louisiana, New Mexico (1 of 2), Utah

2 Alabama (2 of 2)

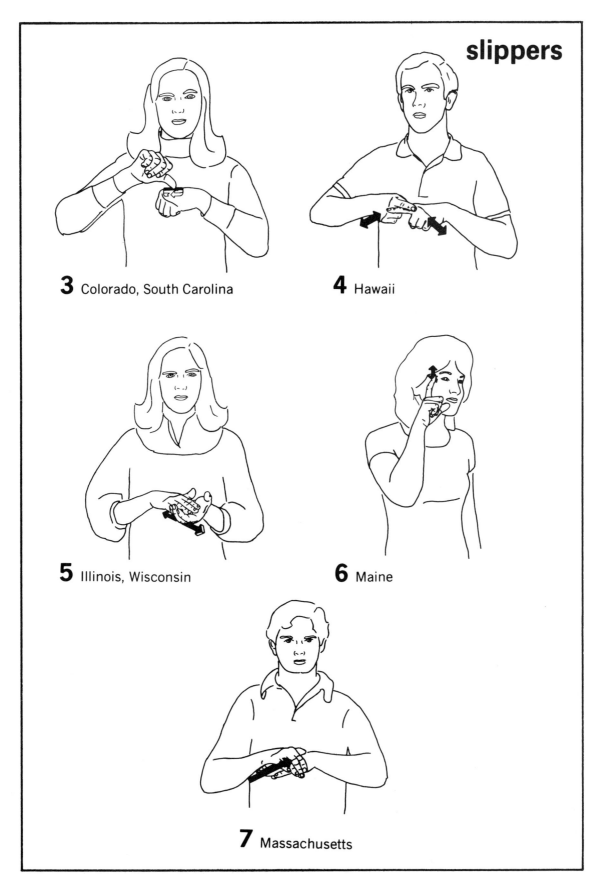

slippers

3 Colorado, South Carolina

4 Hawaii

5 Illinois, Wisconsin

6 Maine

7 Massachusetts

slippers

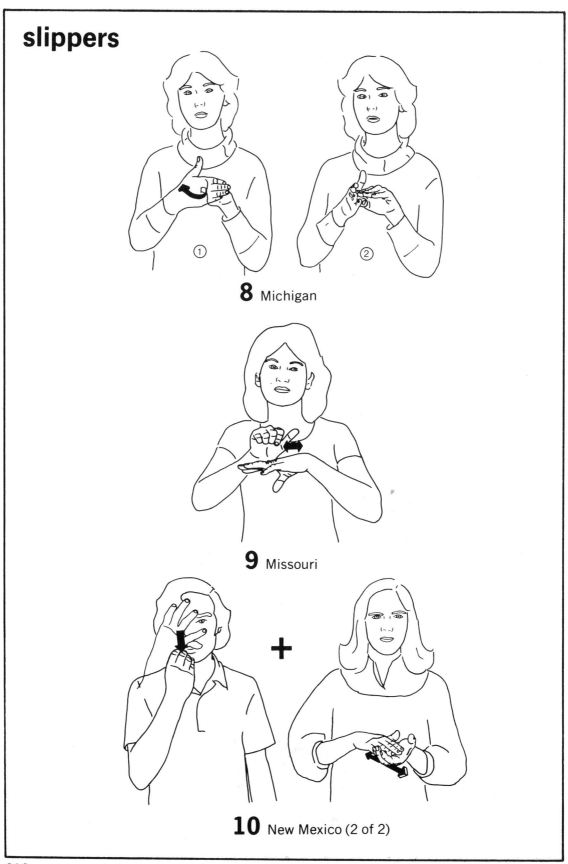

8 Michigan

9 Missouri

10 New Mexico (2 of 2)

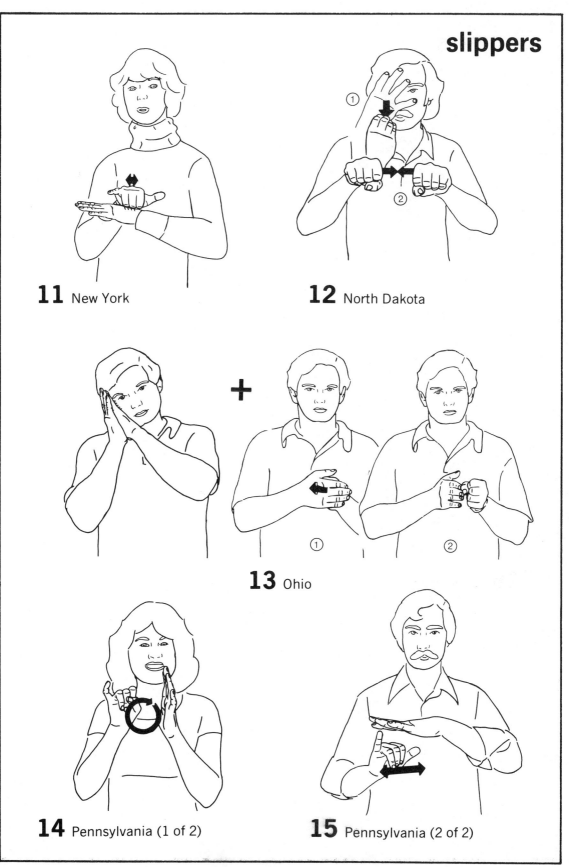

11 New York

12 North Dakota

13 Ohio

14 Pennsylvania (1 of 2)

15 Pennsylvania (2 of 2)

slippers

16 Texas

17 Virginia

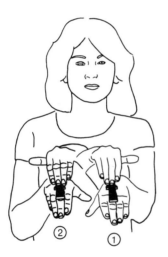

18 Washington

212

sloppy

Her work is sloppy.

FINGERSPELL: Alabama, Ohio, South Carolina

1 Arkansas, Maine, Massachusetts (1 of 2), Pennsylvania

2 California, Illinois, Louisiana, Massachusetts (2 of 2), North Dakota, Utah

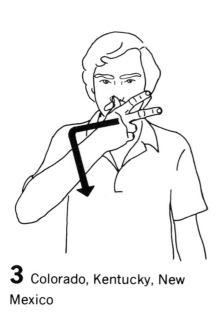

3 Colorado, Kentucky, New Mexico

4 Florida, North Carolina, Virginia

213

sloppy

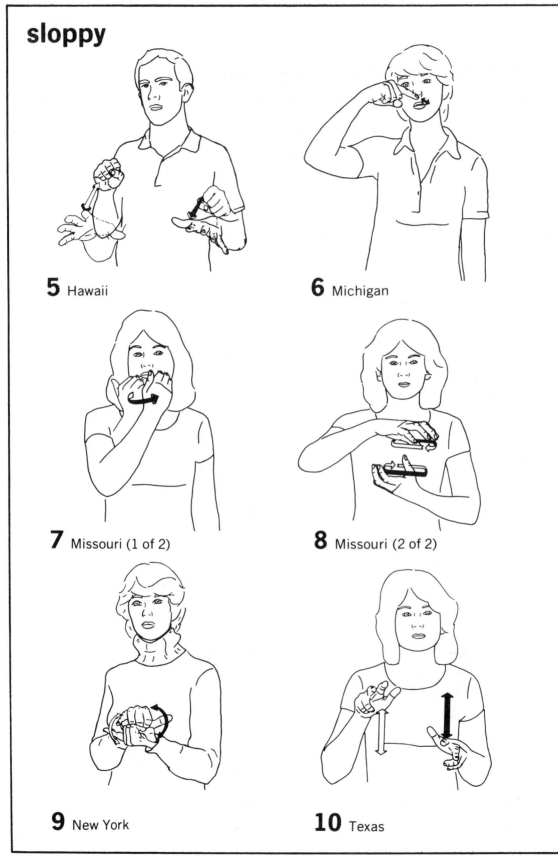

5 Hawaii

6 Michigan

7 Missouri (1 of 2)

8 Missouri (2 of 2)

9 New York

10 Texas

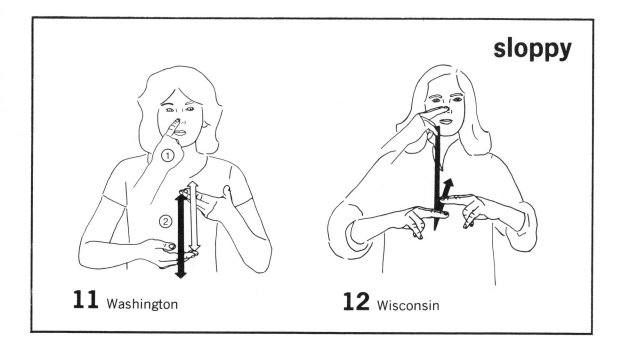

11 Washington

12 Wisconsin

snow   The snow covered the cars.

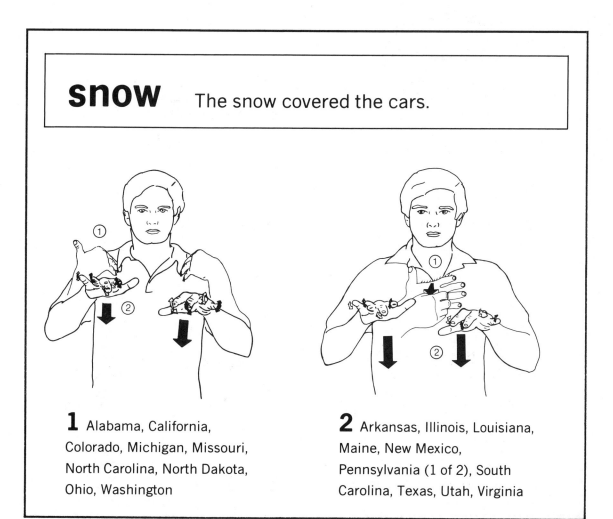

1 Alabama, California, Colorado, Michigan, Missouri, North Carolina, North Dakota, Ohio, Washington

2 Arkansas, Illinois, Louisiana, Maine, New Mexico, Pennsylvania (1 of 2), South Carolina, Texas, Utah, Virginia

snow

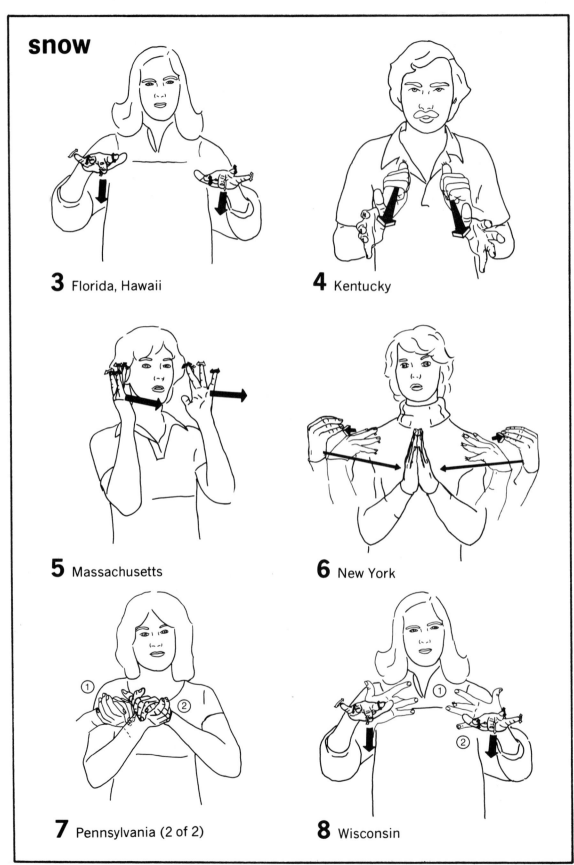

3 Florida, Hawaii

4 Kentucky

5 Massachusetts

6 New York

7 Pennsylvania (2 of 2)

8 Wisconsin

socks

His socks don't match.

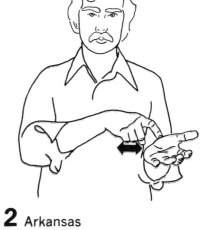

1 Alabama, California, Colorado, Florida, Illinois, Kentucky, Louisiana, Maine, Massachusetts, Michigan, New Mexico, North Carolina, Pennsylvania (1 of 2), Texas, Utah, Virginia, Wisconsin

2 Arkansas

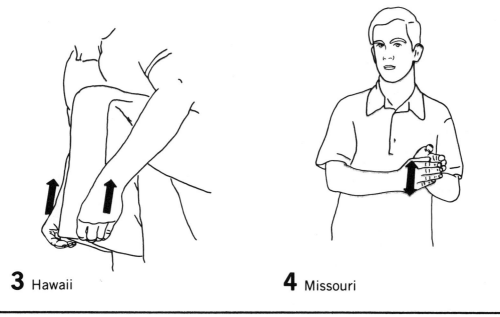

3 Hawaii

4 Missouri

socks

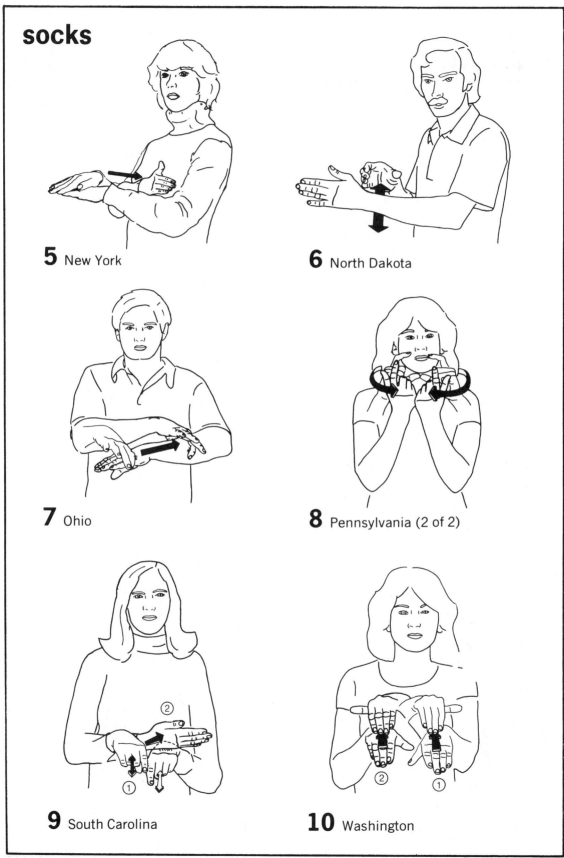

5 New York

6 North Dakota

7 Ohio

8 Pennsylvania (2 of 2)

9 South Carolina

10 Washington

218

soon   I must leave soon.

FINGERSPELL: Kentucky, Michigan, South Carolina

1 Alabama, Arkansas, North Carolina (1 of 2), Texas

2 California, Florida, Illinois, Missouri, North Carolina (2 of 2), North Dakota, Pennsylvania, Utah (1 of 2), Wisconsin

3 Colorado

soon

4 Hawaii

5 Louisiana

6 Maine, Massachusetts, Utah
(2 of 2), Washington

7 New Mexico

8 New York

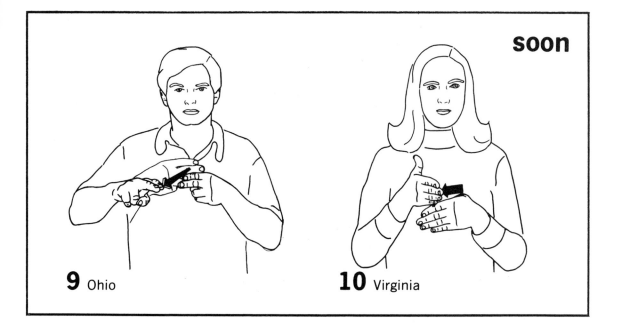

soon

9 Ohio

10 Virginia

spaghetti

I prefer spaghetti with meat sauce.

FINGERSPELL: Maine, North Dakota, South Carolina

1 Alabama, Illinois (1 of 2), Ohio

2 Arkansas

spaghetti

3 California

4 Colorado

5 Florida (1 of 2), Illinois (2 of 2), Louisiana, Massachusetts, Utah, Texas

6 Florida (2 of 2)

7 Hawaii

8 Kentucky, Wisconsin

9 Michigan

10 Missouri

11 New Mexico, North Carolina, Virginia

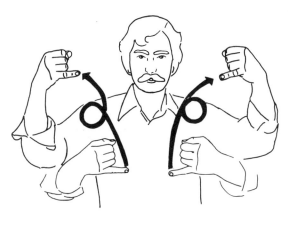

12 New York

13 Pennsylvania (1 of 2)

spaghetti

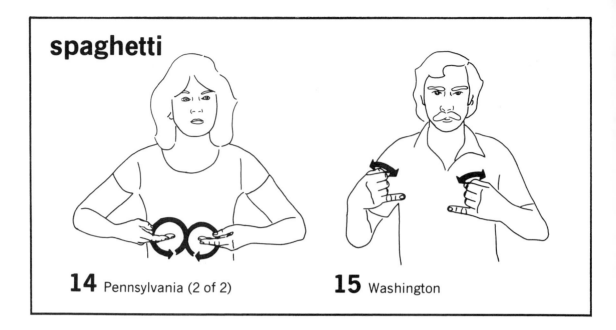

14 Pennsylvania (2 of 2)

15 Washington

spinach

The chef put crumbled bacon in the spinach salad.

FINGERSPELL: Alabama, California, Colorado, Florida, Illinois, Kentucky, Louisiana, Maine, Michigan, New Mexico, North Carolina, North Dakota, Ohio, South Carolina, Utah, Virginia, Washington, Wisconsin

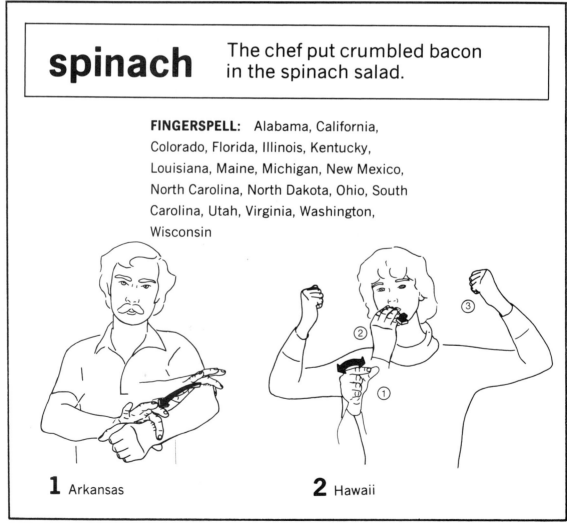

1 Arkansas

2 Hawaii

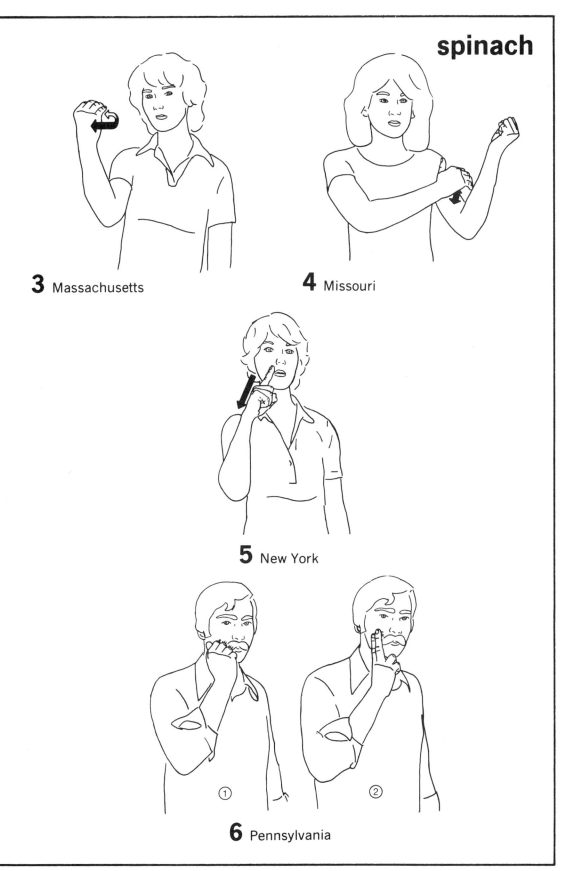

spinach

3 Massachusetts

4 Missouri

5 New York

6 Pennsylvania

spinach

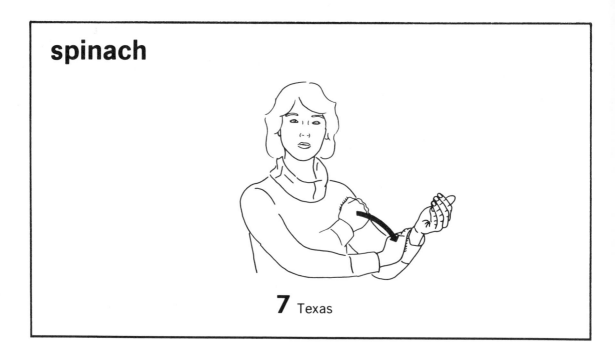

7 Texas

squirrel They went squirrel hunting.

1 Alabama, California

2 Arkansas, Colorado,
Louisiana, Massachusetts, Texas

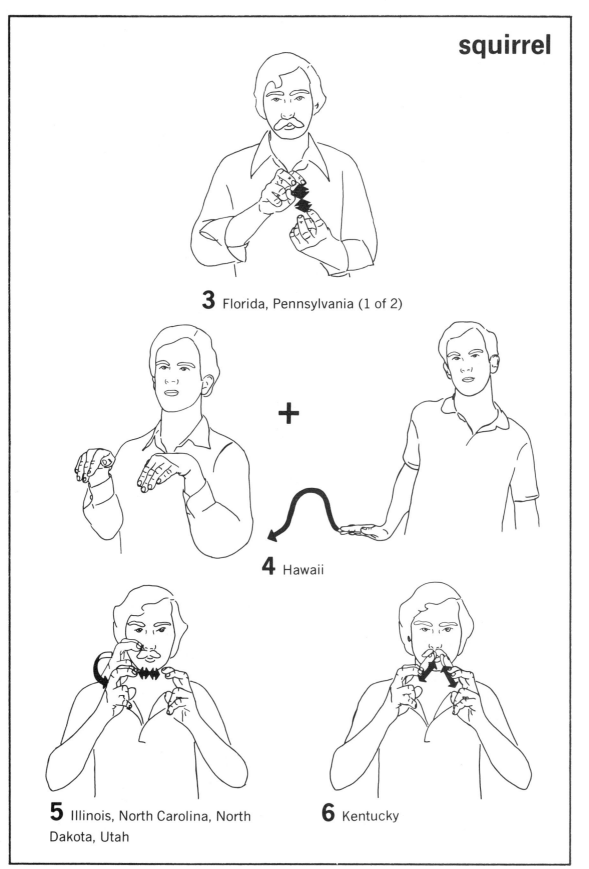

3 Florida, Pennsylvania (1 of 2)

+

4 Hawaii

5 Illinois, North Carolina, North Dakota, Utah

6 Kentucky

squirrel

7 Maine

8 Michigan, Ohio

9 Missouri

10 New Mexico

11 New York

12 Pennsylvania (2 of 2)

13 South Carolina

14 Virginia

15 Washington

16 Wisconsin

station

The train station is crowded every Friday night.

FINGERSPELL: Alabama, Arkansas, California, Colorado, Illinois, Louisiana, Maine, Michigan, North Carolina, Ohio, South Carolina, Texas, Utah, Virginia, Wisconsin

1 Florida

2 Hawaii

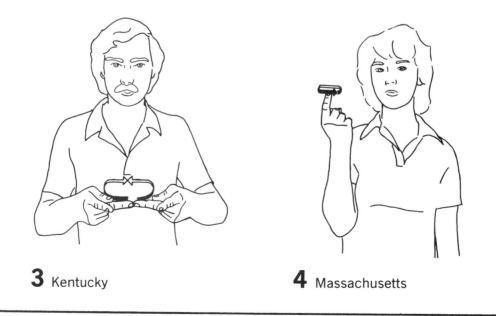

3 Kentucky

4 Massachusetts

5 Missouri

+

6 New Mexico

7 New York

8 North Dakota

station

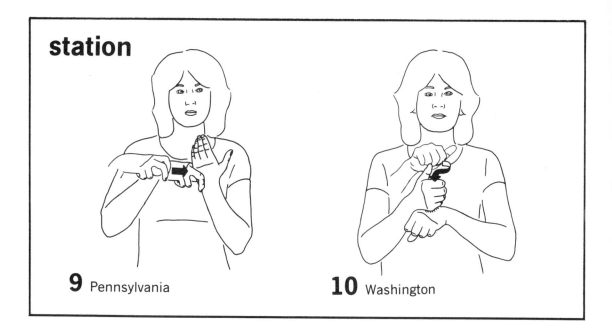

9 Pennsylvania

10 Washington

stone   I have a stone in my shoe.

FINGERSPELL: California, Virginia

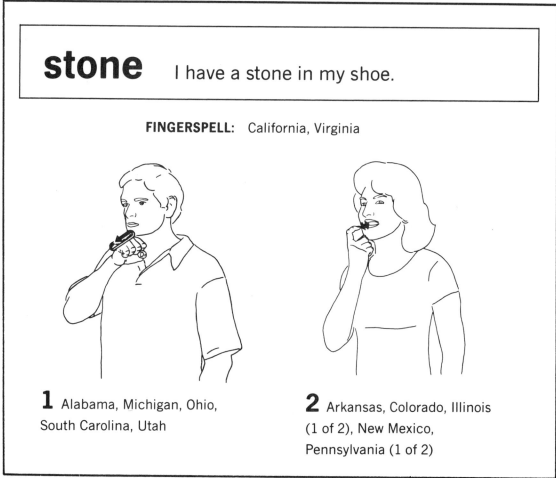

1 Alabama, Michigan, Ohio, South Carolina, Utah

2 Arkansas, Colorado, Illinois (1 of 2), New Mexico, Pennsylvania (1 of 2)

stone

3 Florida, Illinois (2 of 2), North Carolina

4 Hawaii

5 Kentucky, Louisiana, Missouri, Pennsylvania (2 of 2), Texas, Washington, Wisconsin

6 Maine, North Dakota

7 Massachusetts

8 New York

The store opens at 10:00 a.m. Monday through Saturday.

1 Alabama, California, Colorado, Florida, Illinois, Kentucky, Louisiana, Massachusetts (1 of 2), Michigan, Missouri, New Mexico, New York, North Carolina (1 of 2), North Dakota, Ohio, Pennsylvania (1 of 3), Texas, Utah, Washington, Wisconsin

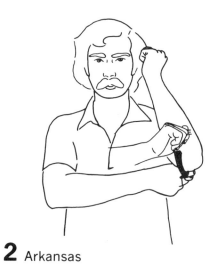

2 Arkansas

3 Hawaii

4 Maine

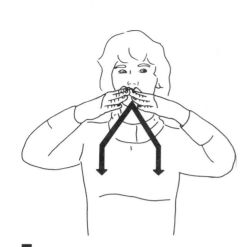

5 Massachusetts (2 of 2)

6 North Carolina (2 of 2)

7 Pennsylvania (2 of 3)

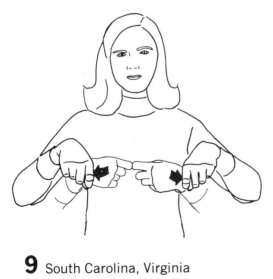

8 Pennsylvania (3 of 3)

9 South Carolina, Virginia

strawberry

He likes strawberry jam.

FINGERSPELL: Michigan, North Dakota, Ohio, Texas

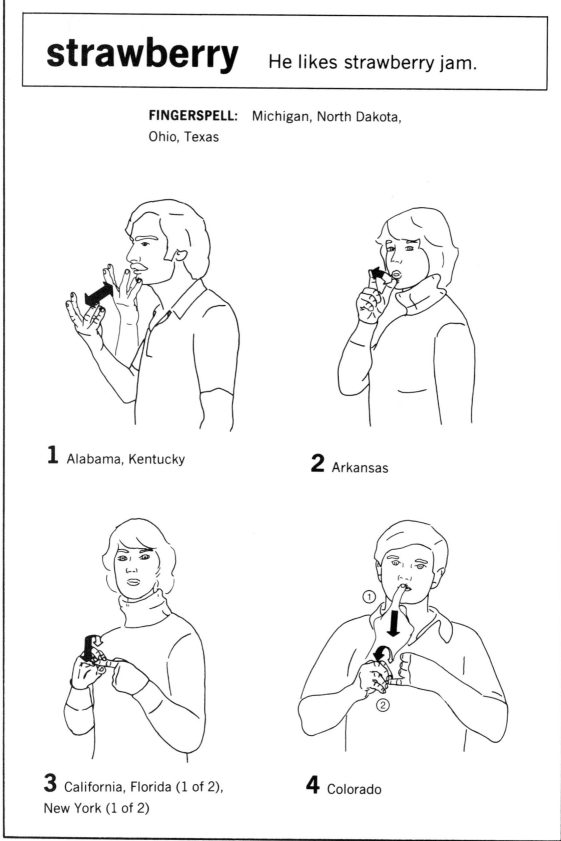

1 Alabama, Kentucky

2 Arkansas

3 California, Florida (1 of 2), New York (1 of 2)

4 Colorado

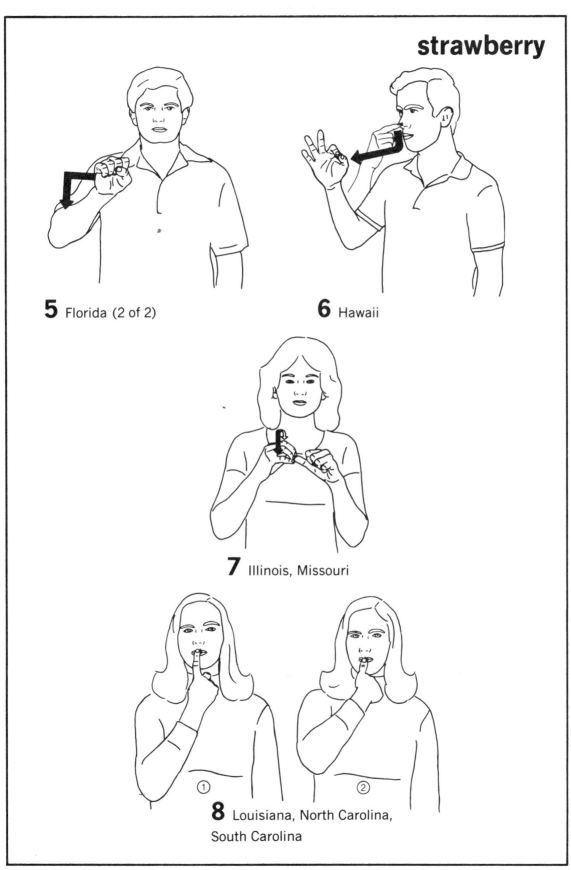

5 Florida (2 of 2)

6 Hawaii

7 Illinois, Missouri

① ②

8 Louisiana, North Carolina, South Carolina

strawberry

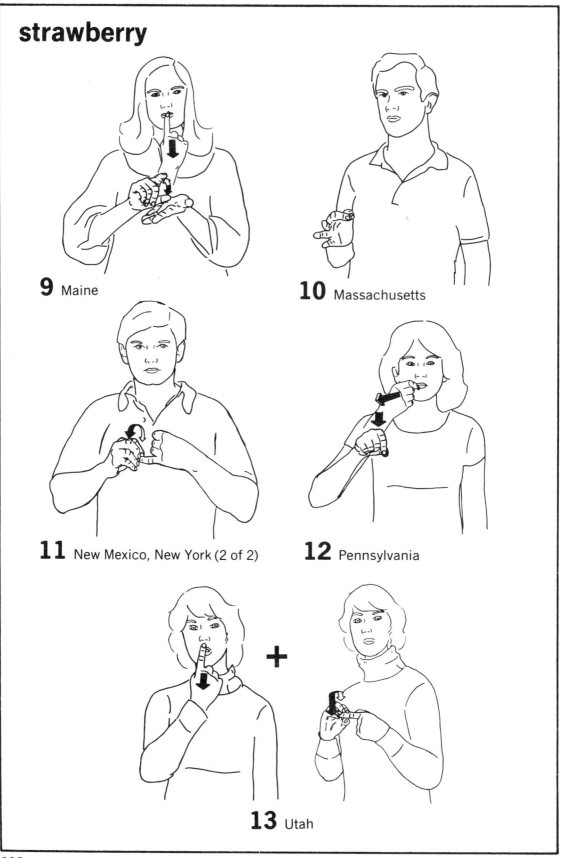

9 Maine

10 Massachusetts

11 New Mexico, New York (2 of 2)

12 Pennsylvania

13 Utah

14 Virginia

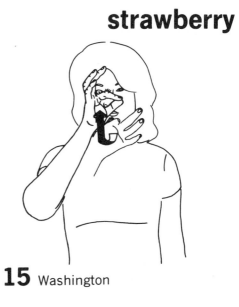

15 Washington

16 Wisconsin

Sunday

Sunday is my day of rest.

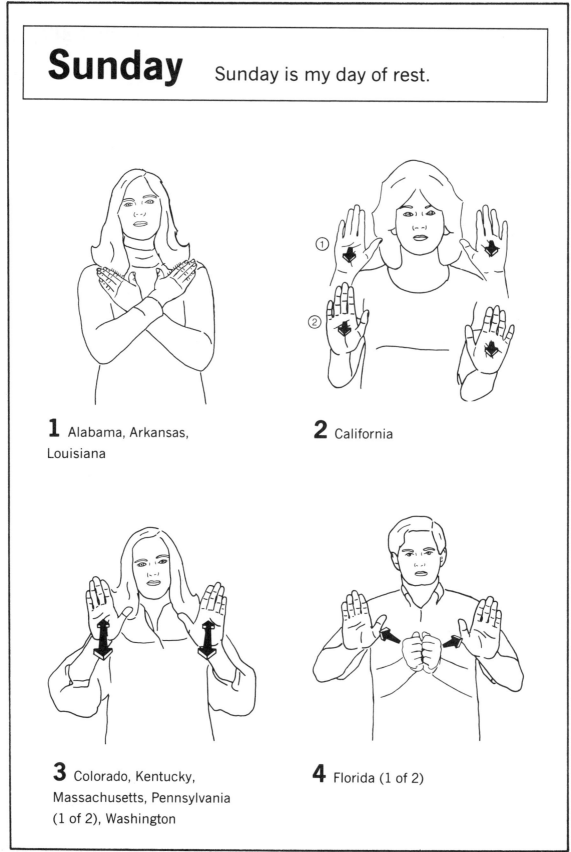

1 Alabama, Arkansas, Louisiana

2 California

3 Colorado, Kentucky, Massachusetts, Pennsylvania (1 of 2), Washington

4 Florida (1 of 2)

5 Florida (2 of 2), Illinois, Michigan, Missouri, New Mexico, Texas, Utah, Virginia, Wisconsin

6 Hawaii

7 Maine

8 New York

9 North Carolina

10 North Dakota

241

Sunday

11 Ohio

12 Pennsylvania (2 of 2)

13 South Carolina

tea I drink iced tea at lunch.

FINGERSPELL: Alabama, North Carolina, South Carolina

1 Arkansas, California, Illinois, Kentucky, Louisiana, Massachusetts, Michigan, Missouri, New Mexico, North Dakota, Ohio, Pennsylvania, Texas, Utah

2 Colorado, New York

3 Florida, Wisconsin

4 Hawaii

tea

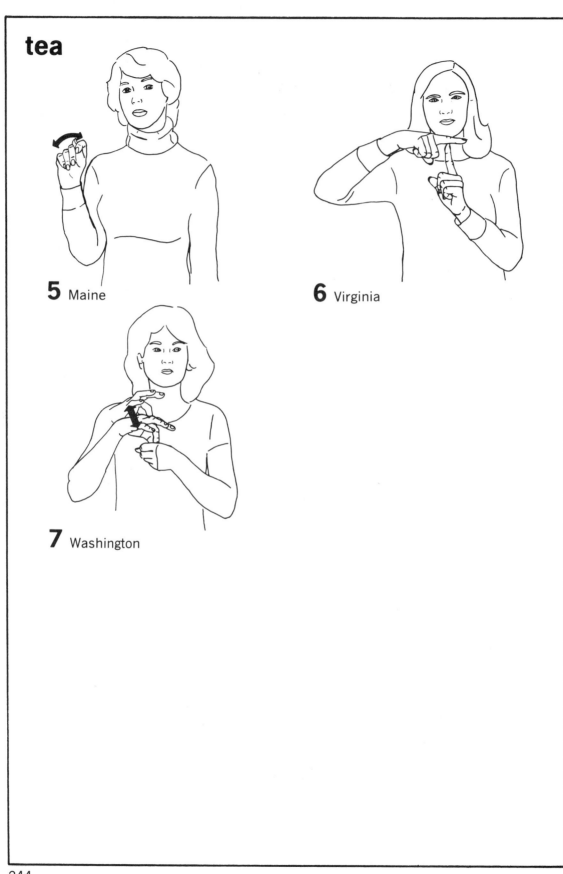

5 Maine

6 Virginia

7 Washington

244

Thanksgiving

Thanksgiving is always in November.

1 Alabama, Illinois, New Mexico, South Carolina

2 Arkansas

3 California

4 Colorado, Missouri (1 of 2), Virginia

Thanksgiving

5 Florida, Missouri (2 of 2)

6 Hawaii

① ②

7 Kentucky

8 Louisiana, North Dakota

Thanksgiving

9 Maine

10 Massachusetts

11 Michigan, Ohio, Wisconsin

12 New York

13 North Carolina, Pennsylvania

Thanksgiving

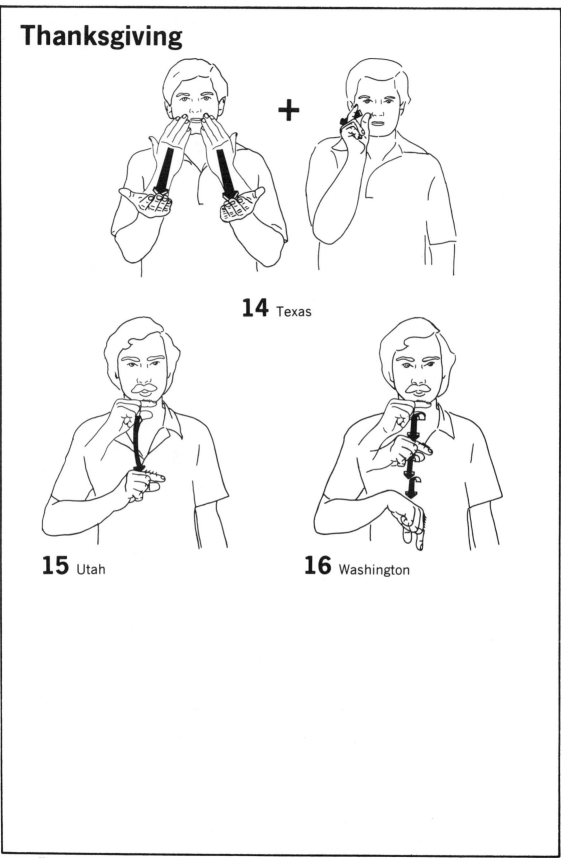

14 Texas

15 Utah

16 Washington

thief

The police caught the thief.

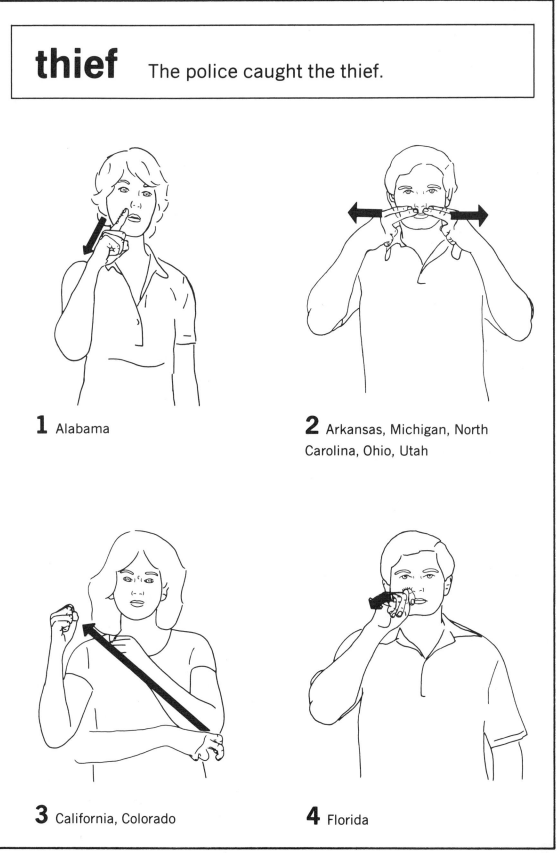

1 Alabama

2 Arkansas, Michigan, North Carolina, Ohio, Utah

3 California, Colorado

4 Florida

thief

5 Hawaii

6 Illinois

7 Kentucky, North Dakota,
Wisconsin

8 Louisiana, Massachusetts,
Virginia

9 Maine

10 Missouri

thief

11 New Mexico

12 New York

13 Pennsylvania

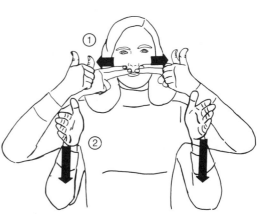

14 South Carolina

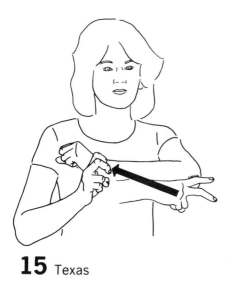

15 Texas

16 Washington

thin

She is very thin now.

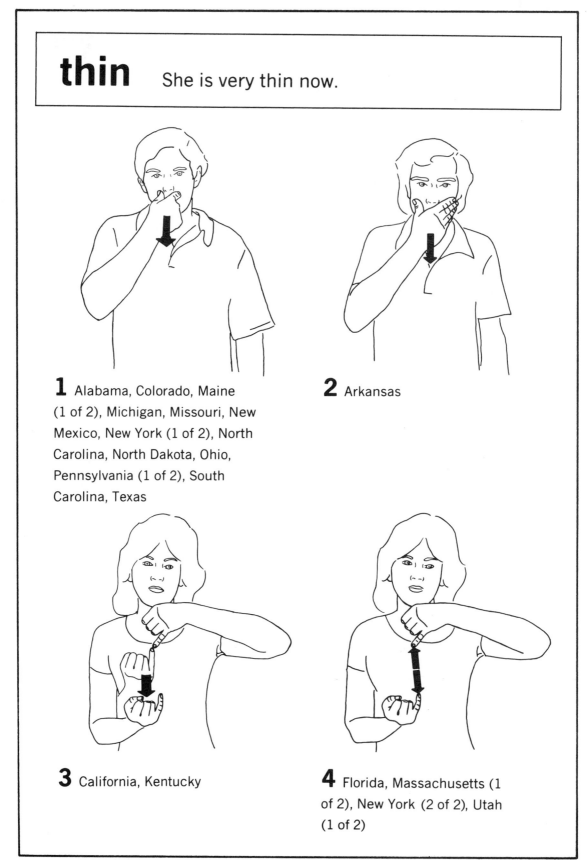

1 Alabama, Colorado, Maine (1 of 2), Michigan, Missouri, New Mexico, New York (1 of 2), North Carolina, North Dakota, Ohio, Pennsylvania (1 of 2), South Carolina, Texas

2 Arkansas

3 California, Kentucky

4 Florida, Massachusetts (1 of 2), New York (2 of 2), Utah (1 of 2)

5 Hawaii, Massachusetts (2 of 2)

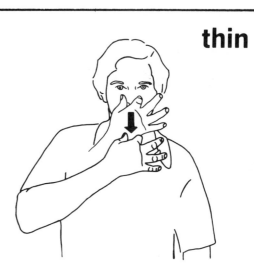

6 Illinois

7 Louisiana, Utah (2 of 2),
Wisconsin

8 Maine (2 of 2), Pennsylvania
(2 of 2) Virginia

9 Washington

Thursday

She went to Texas last Thursday.

1 Alabama, Arkansas, Colorado, Illinois, Louisiana, Maine, Massachusetts, New Mexico, North Carolina (1 of 2), North Dakota, Ohio, Pennsylvania (1 of 3), Utah

2 California, Florida, Hawaii, Kentucky, Michigan, Missouri, New York, South Carolina, Texas, Virginia, Washington, Wisconsin

3 North Carolina (2 of 2)

4 Pennsylvania (2 of 3)

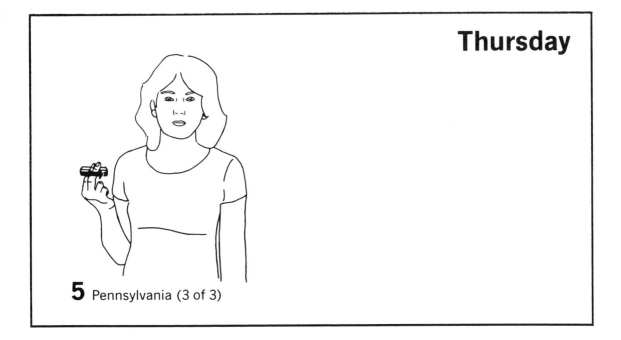

5 Pennsylvania (3 of 3)

tomato   We grew tomatoes last year.

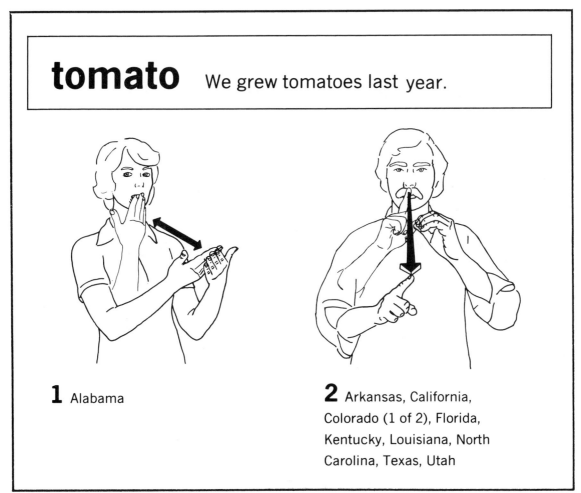

1 Alabama

2 Arkansas, California, Colorado (1 of 2), Florida, Kentucky, Louisiana, North Carolina, Texas, Utah

tomato

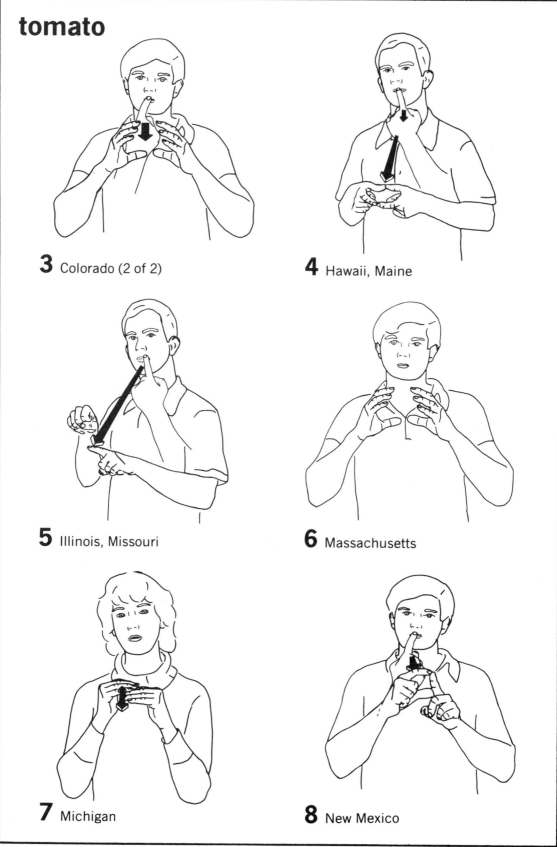

3 Colorado (2 of 2)

4 Hawaii, Maine

5 Illinois, Missouri

6 Massachusetts

7 Michigan

8 New Mexico

9 New York

10 North Dakota

11 Ohio

12 Pennsylvania (1 of 2)

13 Pennsylvania (2 of 2)

14 South Carolina

tomato

15 Virginia

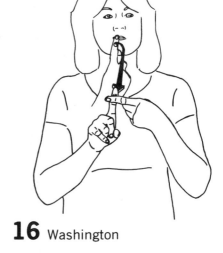

16 Washington

17 Wisconsin

trophy

Our team won the soccer trophy.

FINGERSPELL: Maine, North Carolina, South Carolina

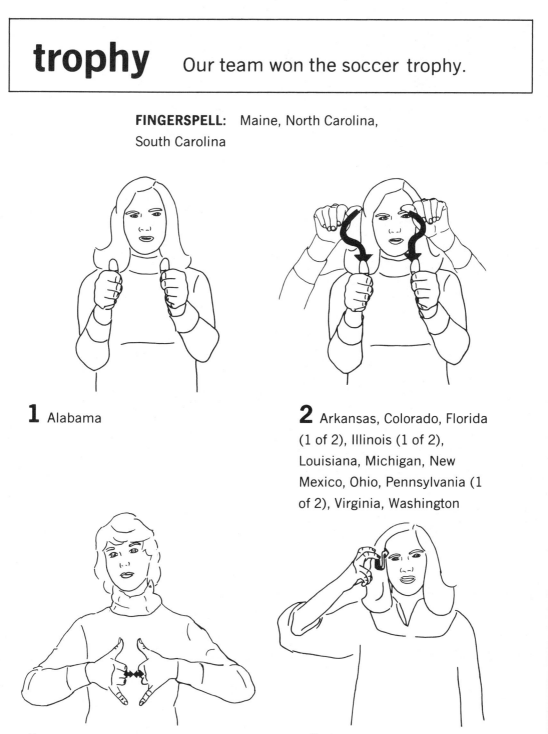

1 Alabama

2 Arkansas, Colorado, Florida (1 of 2), Illinois (1 of 2), Louisiana, Michigan, New Mexico, Ohio, Pennsylvania (1 of 2), Virginia, Washington

3 California, Illinois (2 of 2), New York, Massachusetts, Pennsylvania (2 of 2), Texas, Utah, Wisconsin

4 Florida (2 of 2)

trophy

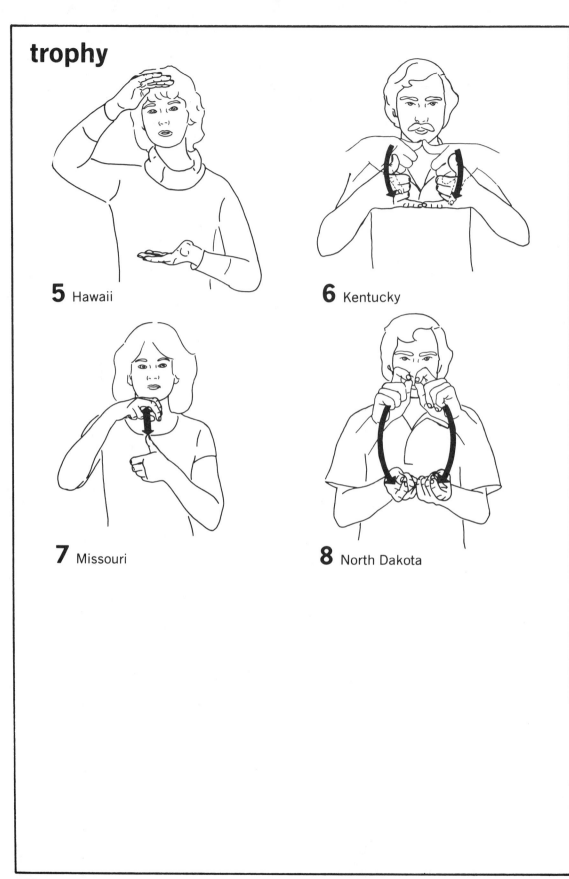

5 Hawaii

6 Kentucky

7 Missouri

8 North Dakota

truck

He drives a delivery truck.

FINGERSPELL: Alabama, California, Michigan, New Mexico, North Dakota, Ohio, South Carolina, Texas, Washington

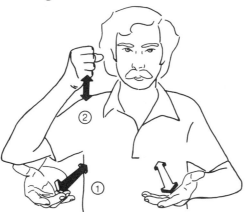

1 Arkansas

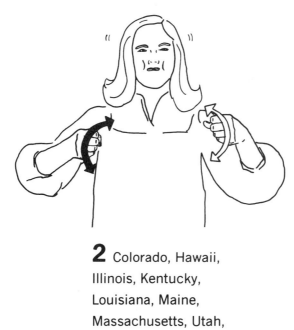

2 Colorado, Hawaii, Illinois, Kentucky, Louisiana, Maine, Massachusetts, Utah, Virginia, Wisconsin

truck

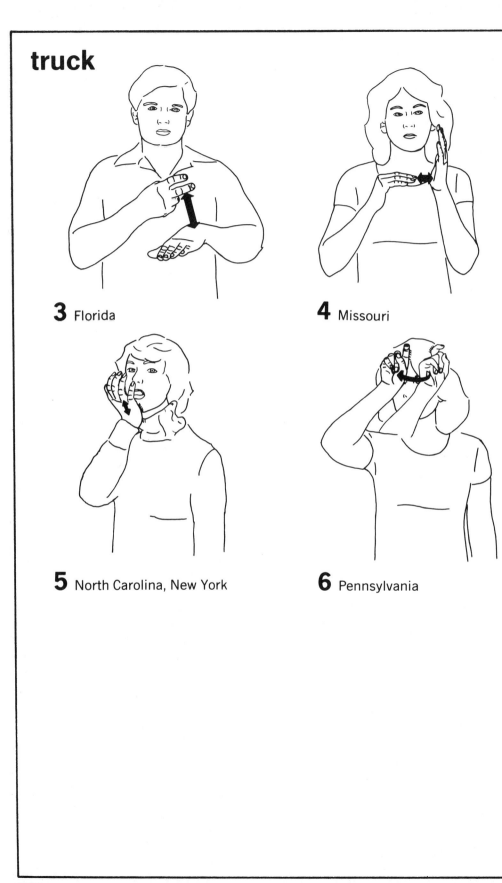

3 Florida

4 Missouri

5 North Carolina, New York

6 Pennsylvania

Tuesday

I saw him Tuesday.

1 Alabama, Arkansas, California, Colorado, Florida, Illinois, Kentucky, Louisiana, Maine, Massachusetts, Michigan, Missouri, New Mexico, New York, North Carolina (1 of 2), North Dakota, Ohio, Pennsylvania, South Carolina, Texas, Utah, Virginia, Washington, Wisconsin

2 Hawaii

3 North Carolina (2 of 2)

turkey

We saw a wild turkey in the woods.

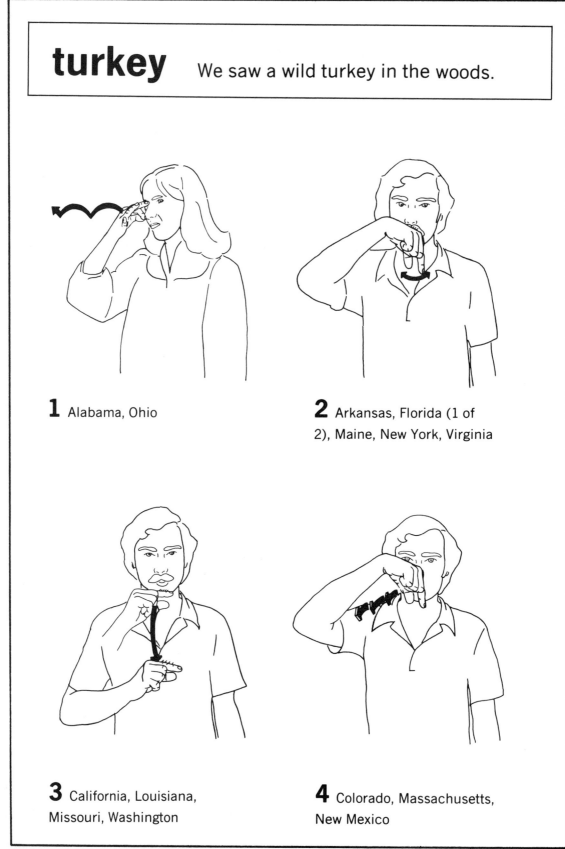

1 Alabama, Ohio

2 Arkansas, Florida (1 of 2), Maine, New York, Virginia

3 California, Louisiana, Missouri, Washington

4 Colorado, Massachusetts, New Mexico

5 Florida (2 of 2)

6 Hawaii

7 Illinois

8 Kentucky, North Dakota

9 Michigan, North Carolina, South Carolina

10 Pennsylvania, Wisconsin

turkey

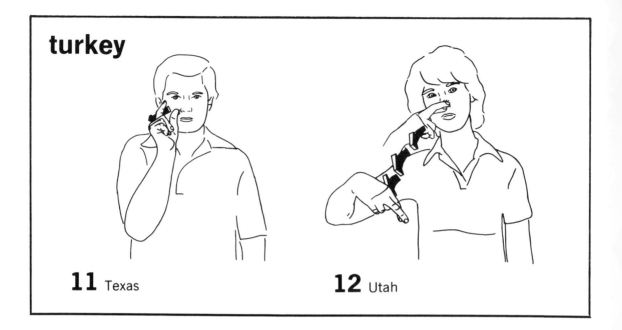

11 Texas **12** Utah

ugly   Her dog is ugly.

1 Alabama

2 Arkansas, California, Kentucky, North Carolina, North Dakota, Pennsylvania (1 of 2), Texas (1 of 2)

ugly

3 Colorado

4 Florida, Illinois,
Louisiana, Massachusetts,
New Mexico, Wisconsin

5 Hawaii

6 Maine

7 Michigan, Ohio

ugly

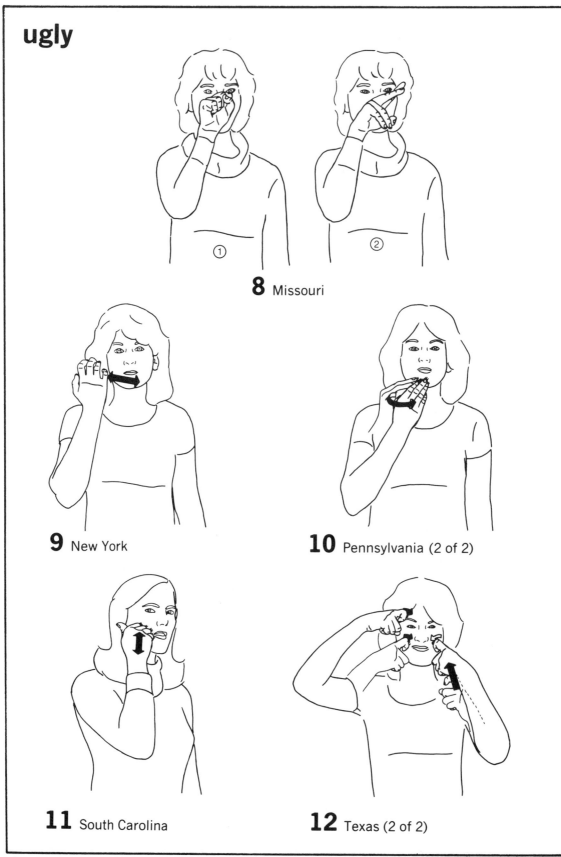

8 Missouri

9 New York

10 Pennsylvania (2 of 2)

11 South Carolina

12 Texas (2 of 2)

13 Utah (1 of 2)

14 Utah (2 of 2)

15 Virginia

16 Washington

watch   Do you watch much TV?

1 Alabama, Arkansas (1 of 2), California (1 of 2), Maine, Massachusetts, North Dakota, Pennsylvania

2 Arkansas (2 of 2), Florida

3 California (2 of 2), Kentucky, New Mexico

4 Colorado, Utah

watch

5 Hawaii

6 Illinois

7 Louisiana, Missouri, New York, North Carolina, South Carolina, Texas, Virginia, Washington, Wisconsin

8 Michigan

9 Ohio

water

The cat drank a lot of water today.

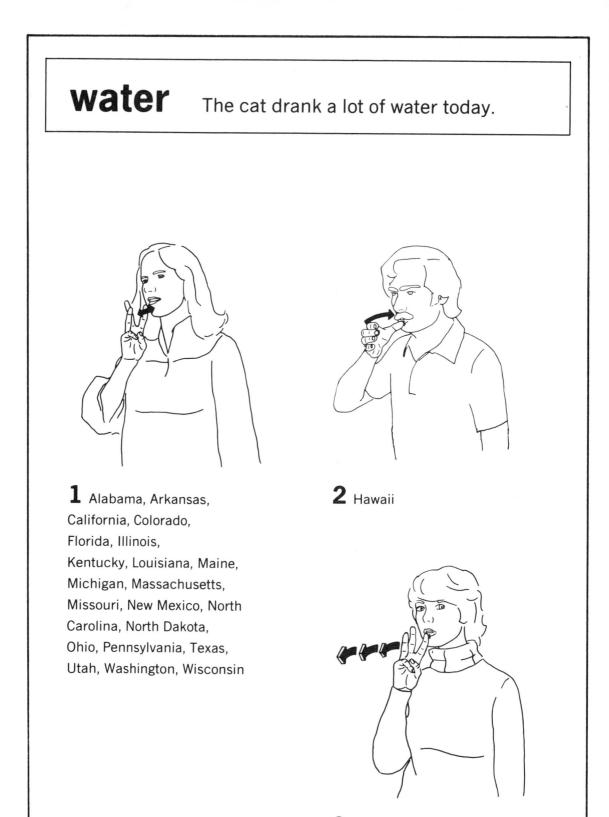

1 Alabama, Arkansas, California, Colorado, Florida, Illinois, Kentucky, Louisiana, Maine, Michigan, Massachusetts, Missouri, New Mexico, North Carolina, North Dakota, Ohio, Pennsylvania, Texas, Utah, Washington, Wisconsin

2 Hawaii

3 New York, South Carolina, Virgina

Wednesday

I play tennis on Wednesday.

1 Alabama, Arkansas, California, Colorado, Florida, Illinois, Kentucky, Louisiana, Maine, Massachusetts, Michigan, Missouri, New York, New Mexico, North Carolina (1 of 2), North Dakota, Ohio, Pennsylvania, South Carolina, Texas, Utah, Virginia, Washington, Wisconsin

2 Hawaii

3 North Carolina (2 of 2)

weigh

How much do you weigh?

1 Alabama, Arkansas, California, Colorado, Florida, Illinois, Kentucky, Louisiana, Massachusetts, Michigan, Missouri, New Mexico, North Dakota, Ohio, Texas, Utah, Washington, Wisconsin

2 Hawaii

3 Maine, New York, Pennsylvania (1 of 2)

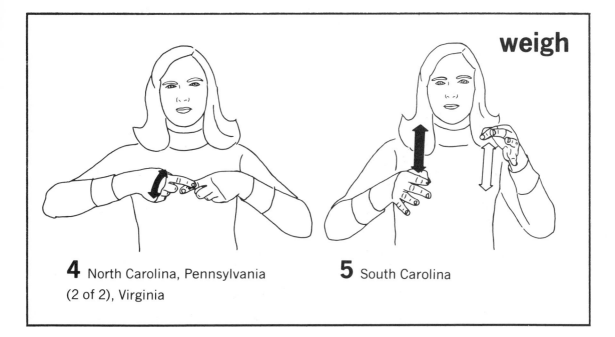

weigh

4 North Carolina, Pennsylvania (2 of 2), Virginia

5 South Carolina

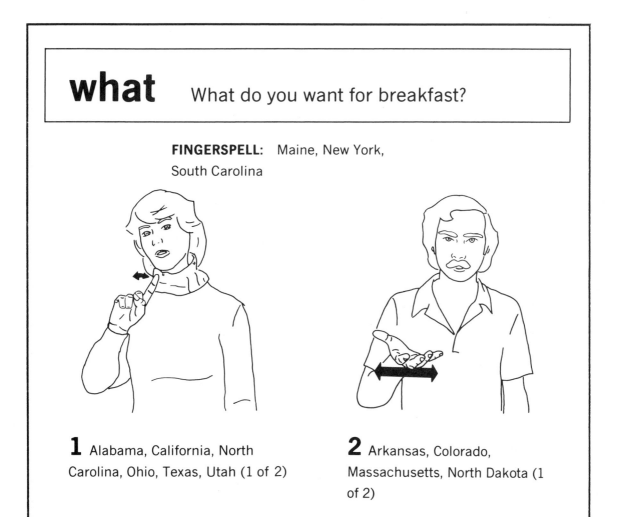

what What do you want for breakfast?

FINGERSPELL: Maine, New York, South Carolina

1 Alabama, California, North Carolina, Ohio, Texas, Utah (1 of 2)

2 Arkansas, Colorado, Massachusetts, North Dakota (1 of 2)

what

3 Florida, Illinois (1 of 2), Kentucky, Michigan, Missouri, New Mexico, Pennsylvania (1 of 2), Utah (2 of 2), Washington, Wisconsin

4 Hawaii, Illinois (2 of 2), Louisiana, North Dakota (2 of 2), Virginia

5 Pennsylvania (2 of 2)

when
When is she coming for a visit?

FINGERSPELL: Alabama, Maine

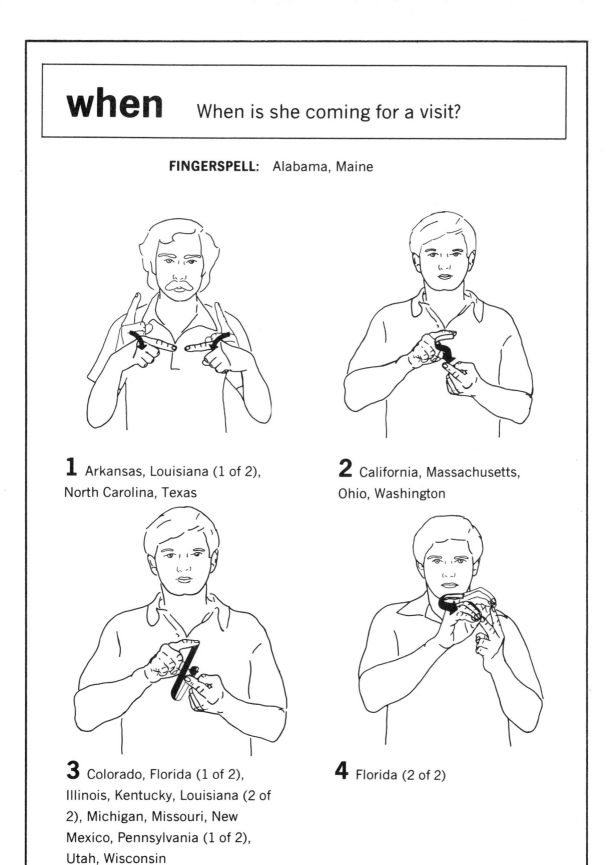

1 Arkansas, Louisiana (1 of 2), North Carolina, Texas

2 California, Massachusetts, Ohio, Washington

3 Colorado, Florida (1 of 2), Illinois, Kentucky, Louisiana (2 of 2), Michigan, Missouri, New Mexico, Pennsylvania (1 of 2), Utah, Wisconsin

4 Florida (2 of 2)

when

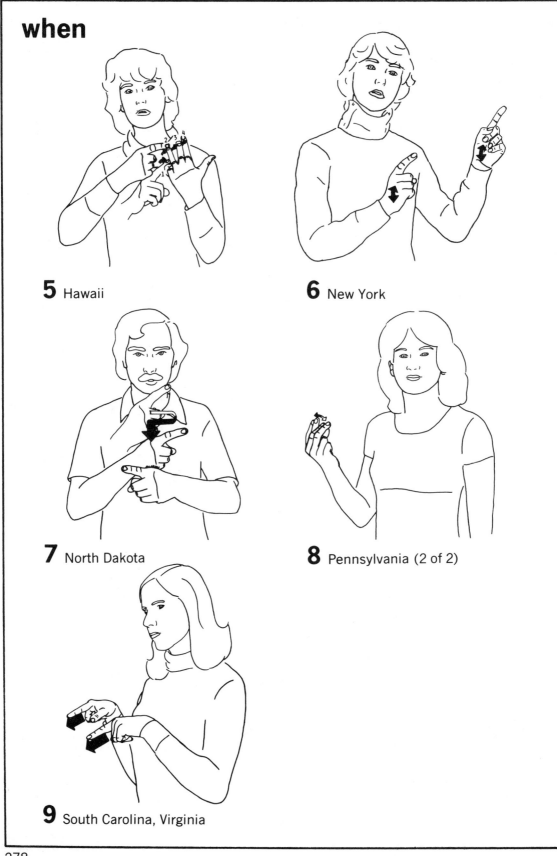

5 Hawaii

6 New York

7 North Dakota

8 Pennsylvania (2 of 2)

9 South Carolina, Virginia

where

Where is the phone book?

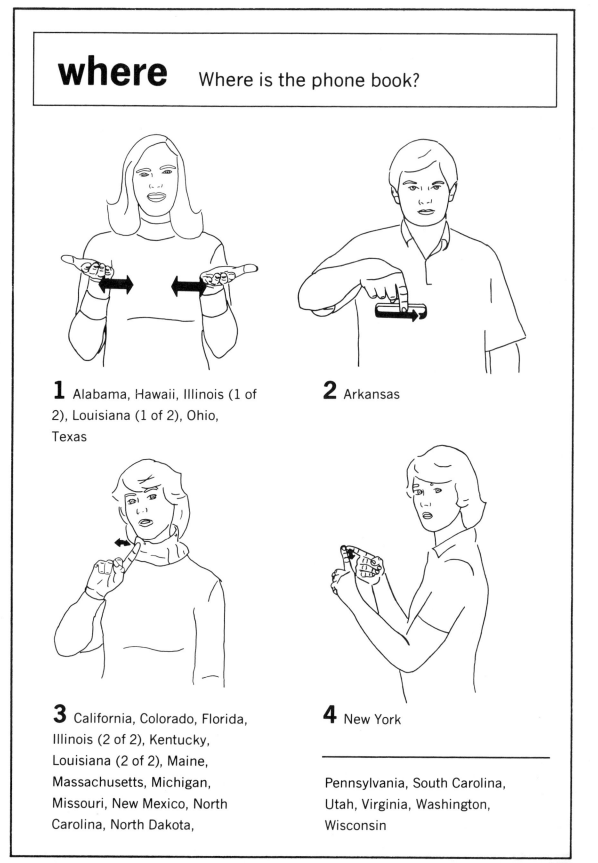

1 Alabama, Hawaii, Illinois (1 of 2), Louisiana (1 of 2), Ohio, Texas

2 Arkansas

3 California, Colorado, Florida, Illinois (2 of 2), Kentucky, Louisiana (2 of 2), Maine, Massachusetts, Michigan, Missouri, New Mexico, North Carolina, North Dakota,

4 New York

Pennsylvania, South Carolina, Utah, Virginia, Washington, Wisconsin

who

Who killed the man?

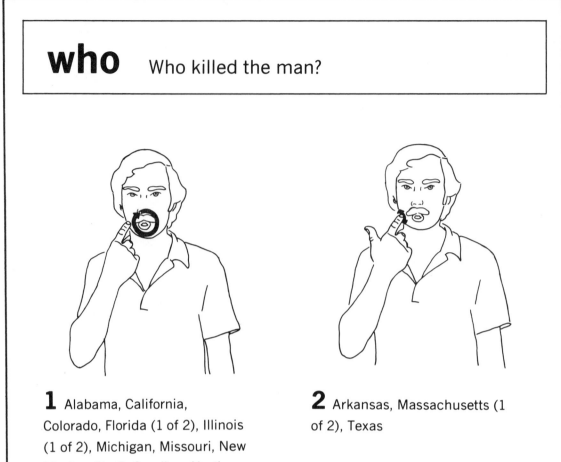

1 Alabama, California, Colorado, Florida (1 of 2), Illinois (1 of 2), Michigan, Missouri, New Mexico, North Carolina, North Dakota, Pennsylvania (1 of 3), Utah, Virginia, Washington (1 of 2)

2 Arkansas, Massachusetts (1 of 2), Texas

3 Florida (2 of 2), Hawaii, Illinois (2 of 2), Kentucky, Louisiana, Massachusetts (2 of 2), New York, Pennsylvania (2 of 3), Washington (2 of 2), Wisconsin

4 Maine

5 Ohio

6 Pennsylvania (3 of 3)

7 South Carolina

work

He works with children at the day care center.

1 Alabama, Arkansas, California, Colorado, Florida, Illinois, Kentucky, Louisiana, Massachusetts, Michigan, Missouri, New Mexico, Pennsylvania (1 of 2), Texas, Utah, Virginia, Washington, Wisconsin

2 Hawaii

3 Maine, North Dakota

4 New York

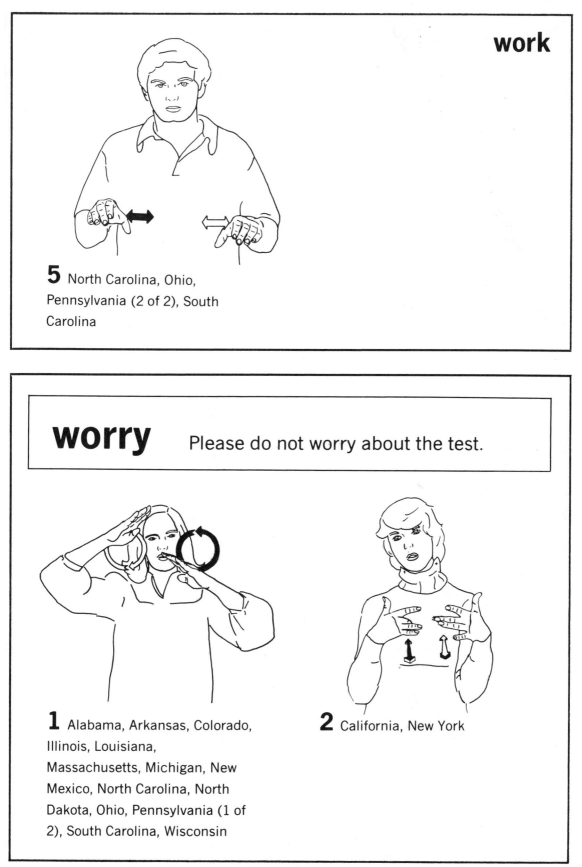

work

5 North Carolina, Ohio, Pennsylvania (2 of 2), South Carolina

worry   Please do not worry about the test.

1 Alabama, Arkansas, Colorado, Illinois, Louisiana, Massachusetts, Michigan, New Mexico, North Carolina, North Dakota, Ohio, Pennsylvania (1 of 2), South Carolina, Wisconsin

2 California, New York

worry

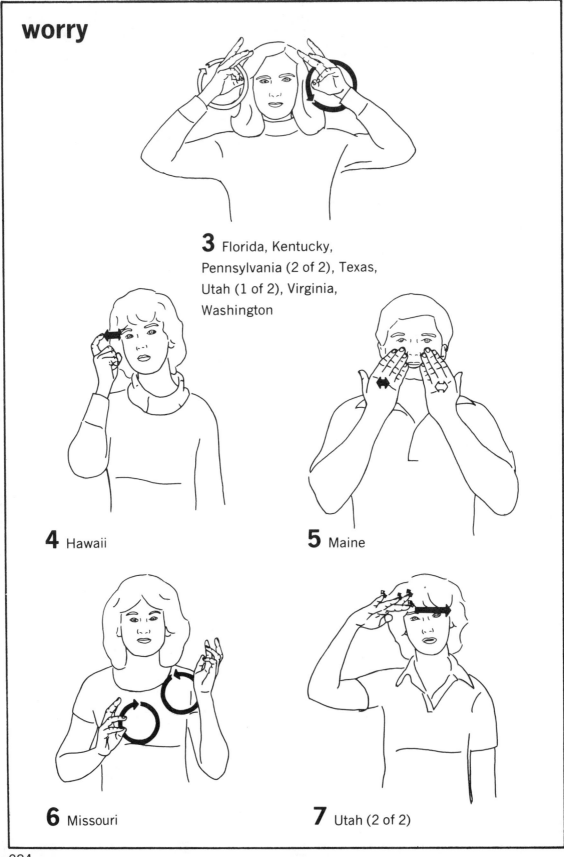

3 Florida, Kentucky, Pennsylvania (2 of 2), Texas, Utah (1 of 2), Virginia, Washington

4 Hawaii

5 Maine

6 Missouri

7 Utah (2 of 2)

ATTENTION READERS

Are some of the signs in this book different than the signs you use? If so, we would like to see them. Send us an illustration of your sign or a description of how to make it, plus a sentence to show how you would use the sign. Please send the sign to us at

1407 Fairmont Street
Greensboro, NC 27403

Thank you. We look forward to receiving your sign variations.

Ed and Susan Shroyer